FAC[barcode T0095162]...

FACADE...

In Every Mortal Lies a Dormant god!

Sanford S. Shuman

Order this book online at www.trafford.com
or email orders@trafford.com

Most Trafford titles are also available at major online book retailers.

Printed in the United States of America.

ISBN: 978-1-4269-5413-9 (sc)
ISBN: 978-1-4269-5414-6 (hc)
ISBN: 978-1-4269-5415-3 (e)

Library of Congress Control Number: 2011900567

Trafford rev. 01/13/2011

 www.trafford.com

North America & International
toll-free: 1 888 232 4444 (USA & Canada)
phone: 250 383 6864 ♦ fax: 812 355 4082

Preface

The Haunting...

Facade, for this word just all of a sudden commenced to bombard me at every turn one day, and it continues to invade my life at any given moment. When and where it all begun, your guess is just as good as mine. Unfortunately, I've been deprived of the recollection of it's starting point. Why it started, I will not be reluctant to speculate on this aspect of the haunting.

I am convinced that it is being imparted to me by means of another realm other than the one you and I consider our abode. It is something exceedingly peculiar about it that I cannot fathom. All I know is that sometimes a voice may whisper facade and in some instances, it screams at me in such a manner in which it compels me to meditate and think very heavily and deeply upon the word. "Be obedient and this command comes from a place that you humans know so little about", a voice once uttered.

I know many won't believe me, but I am going to share it anyway. Some of those of the other realm or realms have conveyed things to me directly and indirectly. They will continue to do so in the lives of those that are ready and seek truth, my spirit revealed this revelation to me a long time ago. Indeed, they are powerful and exercise unbelievable influence. However, nothing goes forth without JAH'S (GOD'S) allowance. Life is a Mystery, and that it will somewhat remain.

This is my Testament. Poetry is my Life! Those of you who took part in my first work and were sensitive, and allowed my poetry the right to penetrate by means of focusing, impartiality, and understanding are aware of this. You are currently partaking in my second work of many. The first work achieved it's objectives, or should I say my father's will and much more. I intend to attract a great audience with this particular collection as well. The poems are similar to the one's in the first book. However, they take to another plain, add, and explain more of what may have been vague and a bit too profound in my initial publication.

It simply picks up where the other work left off. Another link in the chain.

After this, I will perhaps try my hand at another form of writing. Nevertheless, poetry will always be my chief concern and it will be where my heart is.

As in the previous book, this poetry is not meant to entertain much. It is a serious work. It resolves to elevate one's consciousness and inspire you to live that extraordinary existence that GOD ordained for you in the beginning.

At one time, it was against the law for some ethnic groups to read or even show the slighted inkling of interest in knowledge. The old proverb is so very true. Knowledge is Power! Many now slight it and suffer beyond measure. Some even suffer at unawares.

GOD said that my people would perish from lack of knowledge!

Poetry has been and still is a vital instrument in this world today. It has destroyed, built, saddened, and caused glee, brought peace, and many others things.

This instrument has been on earth from times immemorial and it will abide.

Only the poet knows it's true worth.

I encourage all to give the poet an audience no matter what the situation may be.

Death and life is in the tongue. Is not the pen similar, both pour out words? Moreover, my conviction is that the poetry with rhyme and reason is unparalleled!

And Lo! How powerful those words can be that issues from both, pen and tongue at times!

Hail to all the poets of the earth! Indeed, they are a godsend to mankind and most recognize the power of words!

May all praises and glory be to the omnipotent that has permitted me to disclose such work of art!

Indeed this is only my second book of many. I am praying and being persuaded that the all-powerful will bless me with longevity to continue to carry out his work!

Acknowledgements

First, I must articulate gratitude to my master who sits on his throne in the celestial and looks down low. Secondly, thanks to my uncle Eddie Cook for all his much-needed support. For he played a major role in my first publication and an even greater role in this one. Mere words could never articulate my love, respect, and admiration for him.

My beloved and only sister Sandra Shuman in which I love so very much. Beatrice Reese, my dear grandmother, who has a heart of gold, thanks for all the love and countless things you made possible in my life. To see me happy, made you happy and if I was sad so were you. There is nothing I would not do for you.

Thanks for my gentle and compassionate mother, Linda Shuman. She enveloped her children with LOVE that could have only come from ABOVE. Thanks for my wise and strong aunt, Brenda Reese. In addition, I am grateful for her daughter Charissa's encouragement as well.

Frank Shuman, I know you are rejoicing from the heavens.I hope to see you some day!

I give thanks and love as well for my lovely, intelligent, and compassionate wife Dashia Shuman and my wonderful son Ahjari Slater. Indeed, they are a godsend to me, and I am determined to secure our welfare. I love them both beyond measure.

A true friend and mother, thanks Ora Tisdale.

I love you.

Thanks to Fletcher Mills for always being there and believing in me even when I didn't believe in myself. I've never encountered a brother like you and I don't believe I ever will.

I love you Shavell Johnson, thanks for the support. A true heart-felt relative you are indeed.

Sherry Dukes, another valued and loved mother of mine. That smile of yours can brighten anyone's day.

Demetria Mutcherson, a strong black woman, oh how I admire your strength and latent potential.

Nevertheless, David, Renee, Sally, Robert, William and Charlie Cook, Jerline Shuman, Steven Cook, Andrew, Otis, Hillard and Shanelle Reese,Otis and Jada Williams,Alicia Mcneal,Kevin and Danka Johnson, Shawn Clemons, Timothy Greene, Patsy, Roosevelt,Courtney and Teneah Slater, Paula Folder, Rosamond Hinds, Lamont Murray, Aminta McNeal, Patricia Barbe,Kyle and Arthaniel Johnson, Ryan Jackson, Jamie Ansley,Cara Hall, Luis Lambrano, Billy Mikell, May Francis Williams, Jazzi Sol, Luanne Mears, Claude Bacon, Chiquita Hunt and Tasha Murray(I love you both dearly)

Huey Newton, President Obama, Kahlil Gibran, James Allen, Martin Luther King Jr., Amiri Baraka, Curtis Mayfield, and Tupac Shakur and many more!

A Sharing of a few thoughts, feats and challenges...

I would like to take another moment right before you plunge into my world to share some of my thoughts, feats, and challenges. Mainly self-educated I am, independent and redeemed and countless mishaps, adversities, and ridicule I've suffered chiefly prior to undergoing the metamorphosis. Now when I expose people to my story, not even all of it, most of the time, they are usually in a state of awe and disbelief.

How arrogant and ignorant man can be in trying to dictate or predict another's destiny! No one knows what an individual may become or achieve even though it seems as if he is beyond hope or has sunken down into the abyss! For I am a living testimony and so is Malcolm X, who's life happens to be incredibly and unbelievably similar to mine!

However, that is another story for another era that I won't reveal here, instead I'll save it for my autobiography if I'm blessed to subsist that long. Trusting of JAH, I am though, and I happen to be persuaded that I have much work here to do, and that GOD will permit me to be here for quite sometime. Only having obtained a G.E.D. and I have received acknowledgements from President Obama, Former President Bruce S.Gordon of the NAACP also if

I might add. In addition, Maya Angelou, Sundiata Acoli and other political prisoners, Internet radio award for best poem, sought after by some for advice and to help uplift society, and the stories go on.

Also, as one get into my work, I encourage you to be open-minded and not so clinging to tradition, realizing that change in some instances are a must and often inevitable. Endeavor to be universal in your views, seek originality, and aim to be a leader, and unafraid of having to concur with popular and common beliefs.

For be sure to take note of the various terms I utilize for our Maker. For I am persuaded that our father can not be contained,confined,etc. Consequently, there are many different names he is known by and many different ways in which one can commune or seek him. We all must find our places and leave our marks. I will refrain from the philosophizing because my next work is likely to a book of philosophy.

Everyday of my life has become an adventure. How exciting it has become! For I never know what the next moment might bring! I've learnt that trials, troubles, and so forth is what makes an individual and lo! I've had more than my share already! However, behold! Look at what it has made me, so I encourage all to brave challenges, confide in GOD, and endure. Never ever, give up. For one can achieve anything and be anything they see fitting to be.

Now I'll leave you with this phrase that I've coined and may it always ring in your ears and continue to do so even when I have physically expired!

Make Destiny Yield!

Table Of Contents

C H A P T E R 1   **1**

Passion and Emotions!

Notions and Motivation!

Divine and Frame of Mind!

Rebellion and Unrest!

Introduction

CHAPTER 1

Passions and Emotions !

These are sheer necessities that make humanity complete.

For to be void of them is to sink to the level of the beast.

How potent and powerful are these instruments in most instances!

However, one must have balance and permit reason to preside over passion and emotions.

Nevertheless, reason must be accompanied by these two vital elements in order to endure.

One may want to obtain something and that desire or objective may be reasonable, but without that catalyst (fuel) we have come to know as passion and emotions, we may never grasp it.

On the other hand, untamed, these components can wreak havoc and cause unimaginable harm!

One has to perform introspection often and see that these virtues are being aimed and used for that higher good.

Passion and Emotions!

Facade

To me, it seems to be downright ODD,
That mortals would insist on suppressing their slumbering GODS.
For the physical being is only parallel to what is beneath the SOD!
To become that divine entity, you no one should have to PROD.

Facade

What you usually behold is a MASK.
To take it off is to complicate even more my TASK.
However, in the disguise I do not BASK.
At times, myself I can't CONCEAL,
I just have no control at all, over what might be REVEALED,
But, I know most would rather accept what has no veracity than what is
REAL,
Sometimes one is granted entry to my soul and if ready, truth they can will
FEEL!

Facade

2

Love's Bliss

This woman, will I DINE,

There isn't a thing I wouldn't do to keep her MINE!

IF she left, my sun would refuse to SHINE,

Without her, I would suffer a devastating heart DECLINE!

She has to be kept NEAR,

And of any doubt, her I must CLEAR,

Fulfillment, in my life is what she caused to APPEAR.

And for this, I am not afraid to shed a TEAR,

Because without her I don't know if I could survive HERE.

To GOD'S holy word, I incline my EAR,

For a woman is to be treated kind and DEAR,

Being relieved of need, want, or FEAR!

At times, I feel as if I could touch the SKY,

Aiming to be with this woman until I DIE,

This is a reality and no LIE.

True love will make a real man CRY,

With her, my well will never run DRY,

Because she has become the apple of my EYE!

It's a foolish notion to ever think of saying GOODBYE.

Love's Bliss

3

Solace

All I desire to do is keep you NEAR,

Engrossing you in that comfort that supersedes every FEAR.

Ready to assert my love to the world and not just whisper it in your EAR,

Convinced that the ALMIGHTY made us for each other my DEAR.

Solace

All I desire to do is keep you NEAR,

With you, my soul do AGREE,

No longer is it I, but it's WE,

And I must keep you near ME.

For this love is truly RARE,

In such an experience, I wish everyone could SHARE.

Solace

Some utter that love just isn't FAIR,

To testify to this, my soul do I DARE,

Having found one that'll stay near and always CARE.

Indeed this is divine and JAH'S grace is in the AIR,

I can't always see it but I know it's THERE.

From me you will never be AFAR,

No doubt a blessing to me you ARE.

4

Enchantment

You, I do hold in high esteem,

To be true is what you SEEM,

I'm truly hoping that this isn't a dream.

I hope my words don't SCARE,

Beings like me, there aren't many out there,

In your life, are you ready for someone like me to SHARE?

Would you be ready to sacrifice?

Sometimes this blessing comes with a PRICE.

From the world, it is difficult for some to withdraw,

A glimpse of heaven, many times I've SAW.

My life isn't quite complete,

A virtuous woman I need in order for my heart to grow and not just BEAT,

Tired, am I of always suffering defeat.

My soul mate I wonder will I ever MEET?

5

Confession

With myself, I have to be FAIR,
Alone, this heavy burden I can no longer BARE,
Anticipating that you won't mind if I SHARE.
For me you brought a great RELIEF,
There is now hope where there once was GRIEF.

Confession

I know of a fascinating woman, I can now UTTER,
And at times, she causes my heart to FLUTTER.
My soul do she BLESS,
I would like to know that lucky man I CONFESS.
Perhaps the almighty is in the midst of this EVENT,
To find one like you, so much time I've SPENT,
That's why from heaven I know you were SENT.

6

Melancholy

What is this that I am IN?

It hurts to reflect and I don't know where to BEGIN.

At times, I'm happy and then I encounter GLOOM,

These emotions sweep me off my feet like a BROOM.

Should I leave or should I STAY?

For an answer from GOD do I PRAY.

What would really be best for ME?

Into the future, I wish I could SEE,

Wondering is it meant to be just I or WE.

Why am I afflicted so much when I GO?

Then when I return, I feel good only for a while THOUGH,

Eventually drifting back into the state of I don't really KNOW.

JAH bless me with a CLUE,

To deserve this, what did I DO?

Or will this make me stronger and more intimate with YOU?

There is nothing I would not yield to know what is TRUE.

How much more can I BEAR?

This just doesn't seem to be FAIR,

At times, me it really does SCARE,

Not knowing what awaits me out THERE.

It's like I'm caught in a SNARE,

And no matter how hard I endeavor, I can't go ANYWHERE.

I pray to GOD to help me escape this CARE,

Into two pieces, my heart I don't want it to TEAR!

7

An angel in Disguise

Shining as a star in the NIGHT,

In you I see no darkness, only LIGHT.

Relief you bring to people that are at WAR,

Your birth had to leave heaven's door AJAR.

In your presence, I experience sacred BLISS,

When you're away, this feeling I truly MISS.

To you, I would love to CLING,

For there could be no better THING.

How did you become so DIVINE?

No matter what the climate is, you can make it seem FINE.

Forever just remain the SAME,

And in the lamb's book of life, will be your NAME.

8

In the event of obtaining Love

The searcher has to be cautious, but also DILIGENT,

      The one that you decide to render your passion to must be pious and INTELLIGENT.

           This manner of woman is extremely rare today.

You may behold her FREQUENTLY,

But a person's outer appearance has a tendency,

To blind us to that individual's inner DECENCY.

On many occasions your heart may yearn,

Be of good courage and let patience have it's TURN.

           No matter what the CIRCUMSTANCE,

Resolve not to ever settle for only one night of romance,

And never should love revolve around FINANCE.

           For material things are second rate,

Some people allow these perishables of the world to determine their FATE.

The chief importance is the content of the heart and SOUL,

All other concerns must be CONTROLLED.

Deep within the sky our maker resides, so far ABOVE,

           One day he saw fit to compose love,

And here on earth he released it, just as one opens a cage for a DOVE,

Now in numerous forms and fashions we have this powerful passion known as love.

9

Take it Slow

Why proceed into a relationship HEADLONG?

Develop a friendship or unnecessary trouble is subject to come along.

Don't be a rush to obtain a MATE,

It is wise to take time to contemplate,

For what's meant to be will be, it's never to LATE.

To be sure of your partner you have to take it SLOW,

Together the two of you must first try to GROW,

This is the only way one will truly KNOW.

With time, truth is sure to be revealed,

All doubts will indeed be SEALED.

If you advance with this FLOW,

You won't be misled just as sure as the wind blows.

To take it slow, there's likely to be no room left for SPECULATION,

Perhaps there will never even be a need for either of you to make a rededication.

10

Beauty

Most physically attractive woman are often MOODY.

Thinking one is suppose to move on their whim,

Entertaining the thought that everybody wants THEM.

But, every man is not like HIM,

The one who's reality is awfully DIM.

True beauty lies in the heart's CORE,

Inner beauty is what the enlightened ADORE,

Recognizing that the internal holds the greatest SCORE.

To be subject to the external is to not be aware of what you are in FOR.

For mental and spiritual beauty means so much MORE.

To have only the physical is to be confined to only one door.

Women strive to be appealing in everyway like never BEFORE!

11

Love's Phases

What more can I SAY?

Will this all just one day go AWAY?

To GOD, do I always PRAY,

For love, a price we humans must PAY,

Realizing that beautiful things don't always stay,

And I'm just a wondering what it will be today.

Even when love is at full FLOW,

It must eventually come to an end you KNOW.

Enjoy it to the fullest when it's in effect though,

And toward any distraction be like so,

Yes, your countenance will indeed GLOW,

And if the wind is blowing it may just stop to blow.

Many jealous people will attempt to bring your high off love LOW,

About love, there is so much we still don't KNOW.

Love completely, some just struggle to show,

Sometimes only one is feeling love's true AFFECT,

When this is known, one mate usually reaps disrespect.

But, the opportunity at true love one should not NEGLECT,

And to be an imbecile for this passion, please reject,

Seek JAH and maybe you'll discover it from the proper ASPECT.

12

The heart Speaks

To behold your very soul is my DESIRE,
Together could we really rise higher?
Until I find true love, I won't RETIRE,
My affectionate side, very few can inspire,
But you did even more, you sat me on FIRE!

The heart Speaks

Now, do I find myself in a cloud of SMOKE,
The fire you have set is no joke.
Right now, beyond you I can't really SEE,
Wondering if it GOD'S will for you to love me,
        Forever we could possibly BE.
On this day, I confess I just can't take it,
The possibility of you charming me, I just can't SHAKE IT,
I'm beginning to believe that we can really make it!

The heart Speaks

I believe, to my level, you can RISE,
Something unique do I perceive in those mysterious eyes.
Tell me that our fate can lie in the SKYS,

And in me is where your dream lies.

     I'm not the average MAN,

And for us to make destiny yield we must have a plan.

All change has to be for the BETTER,

Things in common, we have to have to stay together.

On this day, I confess I just can't TAKE IT,

The possibility of you charming me I just can't shake it,

I'm beginning to believe that we can really MAKE IT!

13

Contemplation

You're a sister of virtue I SENSE,

My desire to become acquainted with you is growing intense.

      Inner beauty, you do POSSESS,

A regal man you deserve and nothing less.

Outer beauty is a factor, but mediocre people must PERCEIVE,

A wonderful spouse you'll make, I truly believe.

      This woman's spirit is RARE,

If not holy matrimony, perhaps an eternal association we'll share,

The rest of your character, I want REVEALED,

And in return none of me I will conceal.

One another's mind we need to EXPLORE,

How else will we know if it could be more?

14

Who is she Really?

Majesty do I lay eyes on in this LADY,

She could become my wife maybe.

      Are you ready to forever be TRUE?

As one, life can we take a journey through?

I'm anticipating that moment when I'll utter I love YOU.

To embrace you and hear your heartbeat is what I intend to do.

These words, do I want to SHOW,

      And then you will truly know,

That you're a flower and I can make you GROW,

Seeing that you already possess what it takes though,

Continue to look up and be distinctive from those BELOW.

15

Consumed by her CHARM

That smile may eventually do me tremendous harm,

To prevent this I'll turn on my inner ALARM.

Even though I don't know you that well,

On you my intellect has begun to DWELL,

Not just yet have I fell,

I must first be persuaded that you possess no HELL.

I'm not too interested in your comeliness or behind,

For I am fond of nothing more than a brilliant MIND.

Your mind, I truly aim to explore,

Then my soul, through you I'll POUR,

Due to me being unique, you may soon deem me a bore,

But, this life is exciting and somewhat similar to a CHORE.

Or, at one dawn you might take my hand,

Ascending to my level and beholding what is GRAND,

You have to be transformed to meet my standards, understand.

16

Mystery

Father, would you please tell me why,

To solve this mystery, so hard I TRY.

Like an angel from beyond, did she come,

It's a coincidence is the thought of SOME.

Indeed from the omnipotent, she came,

My misfortune no longer makes me experience SHAME,

And on no one, do I care to place the blame.

Mystery

For my life was extremely dark and BLUE,

She came along and exclaimed so was mine too,

Count it all joy and you'll see why when you pull THROUGH,

Upon being exposed to her trials I knew,

That to endure this pain is something I was destined to DO!

Mystery

My heart begun to race,

At the very thought of beholding her FACE,

Bound together mentally and spiritually, yet in age there is a great space,

We seem to be connected, but belonging in another time and PLACE.

A situation, I'm willing to confront any,

JAH has wonderful things in store for MANY.

Only a foolish man don't know any better,

Surly there's a reason why we were put TOGETHER.

17

Love Revived

For quite some time, I suffered grief,

Until she came and delivered RELIEF,

My prayer is that the experience be life-long and not just brief.

Holy matrimony, I no longer SLIGHT,

My desire for love, you once again did ignite,

Rather we become intimate or remain friends I will DELIGHT.

Sight of this, I pray the angels catch,

Surly this dream, Lucifer will attempt to SNATCH.

Love Revived

The cards of love, I no longer cared to hold,

For that's a hand I considered to forever FOLD,

Have faith and trust in GOD is what my soul was told.

Now in my master do I always HOPE,

Passion almost drowned in my heart but a woman threw him a rope,

Truly, GOD sent her to help me COPE.

18

What is that, which I heard?

Love is a very powerful WORD!

So fast for you, have I come to care,

Tell me that life, we will SHARE,

And my children you may bare,

These feelings have invaded me and they do SCARE.

What is that, which I heard?

Love is a very powerful WORD!

I'm ready to render my entire heart,

Say in truth from me you'll never DEPART.

You seem to be so rare,

To not give my all, myself do I DARE,

Wherever you want to go, I'll take you there,

Love, oh sweet love! Those are the words that I hear!

19

Marriage

Our maker intended for marriage to be DIVINE,

It's true meaning, very few can even define.

Unfortunately, countless opt to defile it and cross the LINE,

As if, Satan and GOD they seek to intertwine.

Upon surrendering to this sacred OATH,

There are boundaries that bind man and woman both,

Before commitment, there are two separate PEOPLE,

But, the vow makes you one and somewhat equal.

Man becomes the HEAD,

Woman is the helpmate is what JAH said.

To one another, you are to be LOYAL,

With another, your bodies you must not soil.

Treatment toward each other should be ROYAL,

GOD'S wonderful plan for marriage most people do spoil.

20

My Love

No doubt, she submerged from high ABOVE!

      To her do I run,

When smiling, she outshines the rays of the SUN.

Enough of this woman, I could never get,

Having to have all of her and not just a little BIT.

      Indescribable bliss do she yield me,

And in her arms I yearn to always BE.

My Love

The love we sustain is beyond sweet,

It had to be GOD'S will that we MEET.

      In this, I am in deep,

Eternally, you, will I be able to KEEP?

      It seems so similar to a dream,

But, I love you so much my soul SCREAMS!

And I believe that you care for me the same,

Truly I am prepared to grant you my last NAME.

      Without you my dear, I could not do,

Don't you ever worry about me being UNTRUE.

21

Forever

Woman don't you ever LEAVE,

To your very breast, do I seek to cleave.

For us not to be together, I just don't BELIEVE,

Me, I don't think cupid would deceive,

Perhaps JAH will bless us more than Adam and EVE.

I take pleasure in beholding your beautiful face,

Often I fantasize about constantly being in your EMBRACE.

Forever

There is no need for me to try to be clever,

Confiding in GOD must be my only ENDEAVOR.

Separation, I forbid to be forever,

And my love doesn't revolve around SEX,

The very thought of you causes a reflex,

Her name is destined for the book of love's INDEX!

My mind, you have truly blew,

How fine love could be, I never KNEW!

It's nothing left to utter but I do.

22

How do you become One?

With another, how do one Blend?

How do you not bring yourself to an end?

For this happens to be one deadly TREND.

Some are willing to perform whatever it takes,

Even if it means living a life that is FAKE,

One should retain his individuality somewhat for heaven's sake.

You have to be careful about what you COMPROMISE,

In another, one can become engulfed and never again rise,

Only a fool would neglect himself for a DISGUISE.

To myself, I must render most care,

Of my soul, I have to be careful what I SHARE.

Someone could try to take advantage and me this does scare,

Of losing yourself to another, BEWARE.

Don't ever forget about yourself, I say,

To find the answer to this mystery, I am now on my WAY!

My lost Love

Our coming back together is so STRANGE,

Could it be that over the years the feelings didn't change?

Do you think to say we're meant to be, would be out of RANGE?

      I can't get you out of my mind,

      The past, I continue to REWIND,

Now realizing that the feelings were only hidden in my heart, and not left behind.

Wondering if we could really bring back that old FIRE,

      Tell me what it is that you desire?

My lost Love

      This may possibly be true LOVE,

Which has been orchestrated from up above.

To the present, do you think we can usher in the PAST?

I know I have to slow down a bit, I've been moving quite fast.

      So now, I'll leave it up to YOU,

Hoping I can make myself be happy no matter what you do.

24

Can we Settle?

Lady please pardon me for my MISDEED,

Your heart, I didn't mean to cause it to bleed.

Without you, there is no way I can PROCEED,

You're the one I want indeed.

I'm willing to go to the EXTREME,

Somebody please awaken me because this must be a dream.

But then I heard my soul SCREAM,

"He has lost his soul mate it seems"!

Can we Settle?

I didn't intend to bring you any GRIEF,

Tell me that the affect I caused will be brief,

Only you back in my arms will deliver RELIEF.

I'll give up all I possess,

If only you again, I could CARESS.

I'll walk bare-footed an entire mile,

If at me, you would once again SMILE,

To plead my case, grant me a little while.

Can we Settle?

I want to make AMENDS,
Wondering what manner of potion, should I blend?
GOD, your favor I hope you SEND,
This lady's heart I hope I can mend.

Can we Settle?

I currently suffer great SHAME!
And myself do I blame.
But, to win you back is my AIM!
Because, on you, I can't allow anyone an opportunity to lie a claim,
In truth, I do WORRY,
Knowing I must convince you in a hurry,
JAH please help me to recite a heart-winning STORY!

25

Unforbidden Love

For where went her GRACE?

Of virtue, show me an inkling or trace,

Does this manner of woman still have a PLACE?

I wish I could behold their hearts and not just their face,

Truly against the odds, I RACE,

But, time seems to be out running my pace,

Is it too late? Could this be the case?

Unforbidden Love

From grace, she has FELL,

Will I ever encounter a virtuous one, only time will tell?

For my heart isn't doing WELL,

Without a soul mate, I dwell!

I fantasize of an era so SWEET,

Perhaps only in my mind, her I'll meet.

And on the ground, I resolve to keep my FEET,

Wanting my heart to grow and not just beat!

Practically Bewitching

Is it really good for one to MINGLE?

Many people are just better off being single.

Some women want dollars, disregarding the change that JINGLES,

      Now let's view it from a different angle,

From a woman's hook, man should not DANGLE.

Practically Bewitching

Just be patient and stay calm,

Even alone, Brahma can place happiness in your PALM.

One can't abide by himself is the thought of some,

Due to permitting the flesh to prevail, many are truly DUMB!

      To reality, will these silly mortals ever come?

Practically Bewitching

Why not save themselves the GRIEF?

Some are to be committed to GOD only is my belief,

Not even allowing a woman to offer RELIEF,

For love is often an experience that is brief.

27

Fatal Love

This is when one has fallen quite DEEP,

And finally at dawn is when he finds a little sleep,

Because all throughout the night he WEEPS,

Realizing that it's not guaranteed that you he'll keep,

The price that some women require is often too STEEP.

Fatal Love

But, to see this woman happy is his most sought after THRILL!

And for her he won't hesitate to kill,

Without this woman, his life, he believes he can't FULFILL,

Surly the loss of this woman would cause him to come to a standstill.

Fitting together like a hand and GLOVE,

If you were to suffer poverty, would she be there if push comes to shove?

Pray that our father endow her with qualities of an angel from UPABOVE,

It's not true passion you suffer if it's not FATAL LOVE!

Frustration

Should I opt to be alone INSTEAD?

Having to relinquish my woman for my art, I dread,

Venturing to maintain both makes it difficult to proceed AHEAD.

Will she understand that without my art I'm dead?

Or when I utter I must work, tears will she SHED?

My art I love more than you, I once said.

Frustration

You, I don't want to LOSE,

Between the two, I hate to choose.

I hope that you can stand the RAIN,

My intention isn't to cause you any pain,

From GOD, favor I hope I GAIN.

A great dilemma is what I face,

And my destiny, I refuse to DISGRACE!

Yet you, I want to always embrace,

I know I can have both but only by JAH'S GRACE!

Now is there someone to whom I must atone?

I pray I don't have to be ALONE.

29

Seduction

Don't you dare look into her EYES!
Her mouth is full of lies,
For she is no more than a vamp in DISGUISE.
Look at the way in which she move her hips,
It is enough to cause some men's self-control to SLIP.
Suddenly her breasts, you desire to GRIP!

Seduction

Your eyes have commenced to get hazy,
But, this woman wants a one night stand not to be your LADY,
No doubt, this woman is inclined to be shady.
Look at the way in which she licks her LIPS!
Seeking an easy prey, and of everything, he she will scrip!

Seduction

She possess so much CHARM,
Eventually for her, you will do someone harm.
Never have you had such a NIGHT,
Now she looks at you and whispers it's alright,
This woman's power is out of SIGHT!

Seduction

Though you try with all your might,

There's no way you can win, you have lost the FIGHT.

Any man or morals will suffer defeat or a reduction,

If they aren't equipped against SEDUCTION!

30

Greatest Foe

To be an ideal woman is what she PRETEND,

By eluding her, my heart do I defend.

Too much time in her sphere could be detrimental, I COMPREHEND,

There is always time on myself to spend.

She can be man's greatest FOE!

From experience is how I know,

And countless others have said SO!

By sex, man do many of them aim to drive,

But, without it, we would still remain ALIVE.

To position mind over feelings, we must strive,

A man has to have a woman, what JIVE!

Man's greatest FOE

From experience is how I know

And countless others have said SO!

Disillusioned

Maybe it's meant for me to be ALONE,

GOD why won't you then let the love in my heart be GONE?

Disappointment, I reap every time,

JAH have I committed an unforgivable crime?

Numerous are the good seeds, I've SOWN,

And to only wither again has my heart grown!

Why is it that I can't have one to call my OWN?

This chapter of my life, I implore our maker to close,

Wanting my soul to now experience eternal REPOSE!

And weary, will I forever be of those,(most women)

Reflecting on how dear sensitivity for them once arose!

Free of potential heartache will I be if my heart is FROZE.

Through my heart, many have sent their arrow,

Not just piercing the flesh but also damaging my bone MARROW.

Oh dear disillusionment, have mercy….

32

Hope

For you, I have truly paid the COST,

I continue to fight, because all hope, I haven't lost.

You are the only one I want to lie next to me in BED,

When we're apart you still remain in my head.

At times, at each other we become so UPSET,

But, it's not long before we soon forget.

Together I believe we can achieve so MUCH,

It afflicts me when I can't feel your touch.

The key to my heart, I put in your HAND,

Sometimes you are just downright hard to understand.

If it doesn't work, who should bear BLAME?

For life is truly one unfair game!

Thoughts

My mind must be put to EASE,

GOD reveal the truth, please,

Me, I hope you will EXCUSE,

But, a chance I hate to lose.

In my life, one like you I NEED,

Rather we are friends or more proceed.

Thanks for the blessing AGAIN,

To your divinity, blind are most men.

Everyday, among you, I delight and APPRECIATE,

Individuals like us deserve the best fate.

34

Imagine

This gift is only a small TOKEN,

Associates is what we are, it doesn't have to be spoken.

No longer, will I PERSIST,

But, being acquainted with you is something I couldn't resist!

My admiration, I hope this gift EXPRESS,

You, I once desired to caress.

Perhaps we'll become good friends someday,

I don't want to cause any issues, so I better be on my WAY.

I'll be praying that you find that strong man,

The one that'll treat you like a queen and never let go of your HAND.

35

Muse

Why do you have to GO?

Your destination, I wish to know,

My concern for you, I hardly SHOW,

Yet your departure will be a major blow.

You'll always have a place in my HEART,

Therefore, we'll never truly depart.

Muse

I want to ask you to STAY,

But, something's telling me it's meant to be this way,

We may cross paths again one DAY.

I have never met anyone so kind,

How could I possibly bear you to be erased from my MIND?

Happiness, I hope you find,

Our wonderful times together I can't leave BEHIND,

　　　　Just don't ever CHANGE,

I enjoy our relationship even though it's strange.

To our memories just always, be TRUE,

For I will never forget you.

Goodbye

If I voiced I won't miss you it would be a LIE!

Conceivably, we'll converge in the celestial with wings like eagles flying high,

We may not be apt to encounter each other again on EARTH,

Alone, was we ushered into the world at birth.

My prayer is that for righteousness, we both continue to THIRST,

And out of all my friends, you come first.

I wish you could STAY,

We all have a destiny and sometimes we have to embark a separate way,

Your loyalty and graciousness, I could never REPAY.

Why do people say goodbye?

If in the heart that departing person LIE,

Instead, one should state positively, have a nice journey,

May your life be filled with milk and HONEY!

37

Dilemma

You, I want to so passionately CARESS,

It may be impossible though, I hate to confess,

Only a revelation from the all-knowing can relieve my STRESS!

Once so optimistic about beholding you in that wedding dress,

Dilemma

Us, will the most high be merciful to relieve?

It's not meant to be is just to hard to CONCEIVE,

My love for you is extremely strong,

But if's not GOD'S will it is WRONG!

For a true love is all I long.

Perhaps what we're entertaining is LUST,

In our own feelings we can't always trust.

To seek JAH for a revelation, we MUST!

Dilemma

Could the master have placed love for one another in our HEARTS?

Or before the feelings get any deeper should we depart?

To separate or stay together, which would really be SMART?

It would surely hurt to stay,

Knowing that things could go any WAY,

It might just be better to leave,

Instead of letting my heart continue to GRIEVE!

One minute I'm happy and the next instant sad,

Trying so very hard not to go MAD!

When it's all over I'll be so glad.

38

Hail

While I'm yet living I must CONFESS,
From the very first day, me you did impress,
For your beauty does nothing more than BLESS,
An angel in disguise you are and nothing less.
How blessed is the man you've chosen to CARESS,
I'm so grateful to be a friend, I confess!

Hail

Your beauty many do DESIRE,
Indeed, you have reason to lift GOD higher,
All I want is a right to always ADMIRE.
A queen I see, so of your life, take control,
Outer beauty you hold, now beautify your SOUL,
To make sure you do this has become my goal!

Introduction

Notions and Motivation!

What one devises, determines what one will ultimately carry out.

What one permits to serve as sources of inspiration can dictate various things that are vital to that individual's welfare and the welfare of others.

Extremely careful, we must thread when venturing into these fateful dimensions.

For one source that moves one to act can be accompanied by life-long joy or can bring one's demise, and sometimes in an instant.

I encourage all to take account of their notions and motivations on a daily basis!

Notions and Motivation!

1

Confrontation 1

To me, a challenge is what life PROPOSE,

And from my intrepid spirit is where acceptance arose!

For to partake of this adventure, I gladly CHOSE,

The one's intimidated by life, I decline to be like those,

Realizing everyone has a choice to keep the door open or CLOSE.

Confrontation 1

To be led by JAH is to really be alive,

Having balance and knowing when to be still and when to DRIVE,

At times, too much, we can strive,

In some cases, we have to wait patiently for something to ARRIVE.

Life has a part for us all to play,

Endeavor to accomplish something EVERYDAY.

Ultimately, you wield the power to define,

For some people the challenge of life UNDERMINES.

But, your divinity surpasses life here, so it you must enshrine.

2

Be Strong

If one can breathe, there is a CHANCE,

Death, trials, and tribulations we were promised in advance,

Look life in the face and at her refuse to only GLANCE.

Make her yield what you will!

One day the flesh has to be STILL,

Joy and countless troubles you are sure to feel,

Peer beyond the plain and into the HILL.

Be Strong

I have ceased to desire, but instead I aim!

Knowing what to expect, so I don't run from the FLAME,

And on nothing or no one will I place the blame,

Realizing that life is a mystery and to share in it, temporarily I CAME!

Myself, only I can oppose,

Being a light for some and a threat to THOSE....

The doors JAH has unlocked no mortal or immortal can close!

Constantly in action is how I strike my POSE!

To all, I bellow, BE STRONG!

The things here won't last too long,

To understand some of the mystery is to have an ear for GOD'S SONG,

Instead of always crying that things are so wrong.

3

As you believe, so you Are

In reality you are nothing less than GRAND!

To be fashioned in GOD'S image, the significance of this, do you understand?

For that that one believes will definitely be in his or her HAND,

First, it's manifested in the spiritual realm than on land.

As you believe, so you are

One must follow the soul's URGE,

Of all immorality, yourself you have to purge,

This is the only way your true destiny can SURGE.

Some choose to reflect Lucifer's face,

To be distinct from the world to them is out of PLACE,

Instead of reality, a fantasy they rather chase!

As you believe, so you are

In your divineness, please BELIEVE,

For Satan is always out to deceive.

Why not just open your eyes and perceive,

For one is only the product of what he or she BELIEVES!

4

Aspirations

Effort must lead hope it SEEMS,

This is the only way to achieve a dream!

Aspirations can become so intimate with reality I DEEM,

For this is what I heard my soul scream!

It can be done again especially if it's been done BEFORE,

All your life, another don't adore.

Your dreams, proceed to CHASE,

For you have no designated place!

Aspirations

Cease to wish upon a STAR,

In control of your destiny you are,

And from GOD one must never be AFAR!

Created in JAH'S grand likeness, are you,

Dreams are dormant realities waiting to be transformed, now that's TRUE!

Hoping one will embrace it and utter I do,

But, in some cases there's only one chance and not TWO,

Aspirations should no longer be gray, but blue!

5

Advance

No matter what, forward one must TREAD,

To be conquered by emotions is something to dread,

Fear in most, it was BRED!

Now one must struggle to get into the real sphere,

Being taught to hold fantasies DEAR!

If you don't become realistic you won't make it here.

How should I conduct myself THOUGH?

As one that's insensitive and spiritually low,

If you really search, you'll discover what most don't KNOW.

Let us just look to the stars,

Liberty is granted to many confined by BARS!

And good does some scars.

Now, can I see beyond the CLOUD?

I'm living and learning and I'll say it proud,

Most are afraid to utter that they don't know something ALOUD.

6

Keep your head to the Sky

You were created for a PURPOSE,

Challenges cause your potential to surface.

Life has many hardships to PRESENT,

      An easy road is something to resent.

When the gathered forces of trouble comes your WAY,

The recollection of the AFRICAN overcoming slavery should keep discouragement at bay!

Keep your head to the Sky

Never allow circumstances to be a HINDARANCE,

To believe in predestined fate is nonsense.

Refrain from fantasying about SUCCESS,

Instead, declare it will be whatever I profess!

Everyone has his or her SEASON,

Some become impatient and plot treason!

Mainly virtue pursues those that find their REASON.

So keep your head to the sky!

To neglect your destiny for a fantasy is to portray Allah as a LIE!

7

Toil

Everyone wants to live life in the SHADE,

But, to life dues have to be paid!

And one won't always have everything MADE.

True happiness do I seek to find,

Leaving anything that may come between JAH and I BEHIND!

Happiness really depends on one's state of mind.

One should never submit to a TRIAL,

A day is coming in which you can smile,

Just continue to fight for a little WHILE.

If one persist to engage in conflict, it'll only get better,

At sometime, you are bound to view a change in the WEATHER,

Confide in GOD, because yall can accomplish anything together.

8

Positive Thought

What could be more worthy of being SOUGHT?

First imagine, then summon it to manifest,

The divine entity only renders the BEST,

Rewarding, it is to put the mind to the test.

Only positive thoughts can FULFILL,

       Negativity destroys the positive will.

The condition of thought determines FATE,

In Yahweh's image you were molded, and on this contemplate.

Only half way does one have to travel to ACHIEVE,

For that is the power granted to the one that believes,

Thought usually brings about ACTION,

Be sure that to the positive is your attraction.

Evil has won the battle though it SEEMS!

But, JAH can triumph over it at any moment I deem.

Nothing is more worthy to PURSUE,

Your thoughts are what constitute you!

9

Consult the Clouds

For the thunder is them speaking ALOUD!

And for your opinion, I am to proud.

At me, the clouds do SMILE,

Our relation will last more than a little while.

Toward the sky, do I PEER,

Everything now being all so clear,

As long as I keep my head aimed toward the heavenly SPHERE,

Basking in the immortal atmosphere,

Only by the aid of the clouds can one PERSEVERE.

I will not be led astray,

By being sensitive to what the clouds SAY.

And as the eagle one may,

Rise above the clouds and elude the rain of life any DAY!

There is a price to pay indeed,

But one will be alright if by means of the clouds he PROCEED,

Dreams loom to become realities and on one of the Lord of Lord's greatest artifacts one feed,

For the clouds is all one NEED!

10

Pressing On

At times, I do feel PERTURBED,

But, to cede to troubles would be absurd.

Would it be intelligent to grab a pistol and go POP?

This would only provoke more chaos, and this must stop,

Not everybody just can reside at the TOP.

There's nothing amiss with being average

For recognition, some resort to taking on the characteristics of the SAVAGE.

In my life, there are so many obstacles and barriers,

But, I assigned myself to be the CARRIER.

They must eventually be taken away,

My destiny is beginning to LOOM,

And where there is a will there is a way!

      For I can now feel my HEYDAY,

It's more vivid then the ray's of the sun,

That is reason enough for me to continue to RUN!

11

Nobility

Two wrongs don't make a RIGHT,

That's like confusing day for night.

The good will always get AHEAD,

To promote iniquity is something one should dread.

Victory has a great COST,

But, if one gives up all hope is lost.

In this life, some things, one is sure to LOSE,

But, you can gain much more if you choose.

Troubles are suppose to only MAKE,

To think you'll have enduring success without a battle is a mistake.

12

Valor

Many would love to see you MISS,

Wanting another to suffer failure instead of bliss,

They should be ashamed to even think like THIS.

But, this brings them satisfaction,

Because for anything positive and lofty they never take ACTION,

Now this should be deemed one forbidden attraction.

Their very selves do they NEGLECT!

And the one's that labor to find themselves they disrespect,

Of life, they do embrace one foolish ASPECT.

One must proceed to transcend the spite,

Because some just don't care what is wrong or RIGHT,

Out of your dream, they aren't reluctant to take a bite!

You must be able to see the sun through the MIST,

Realizing that you don't always have to employ your fist,

Their ill hopes you can still TWIST.

13

Pride

Brothers and sisters where is your PRIDE?

Awaken that superior being that lies inside.

You must know yourself, I ATTEST,

This is the only way to live the best.

Why should the conqueror inside continue to REST?

As in the former day's, sovereign power this being must manifest,

For you are constantly challenged and for too long, have been put to the TEST.

Brothers and sisters where is your PRIDE!

Your foolish contradictions and fear you must put aside.

We've been through every possible and impossible PHASE!

It is now time for us to set the stage!

And release some long overdue moral RAGE,

The smoke of the ages is beginning to clear,

And the voices and cries of our ancestors we can now HEAR,

They are whispering in my ear,

Tell our children there is no reason to FEAR,

On an afro-centric philosophy, the children we must rear!

Brothers and sisters where is your PRIDE!

Your foolish contradictions and fear you must put aside,

Now let's go for a RIDE,

With reality, I'll make you collide,

Indeed, upon this journey we'll go very deep INSIDE!

Our destination being where the soul resides,

Be tenacious of your ROOTS!

For no other can boast of such great fruits,

Where is your PRIDE!

You must refrain from holding it inside!

From yourself you should not HIDE,

Let it manifest and dominate all that is outside!

PRIDE!

14

Anticipation

I think about you day and NIGHT,

Dreading the very moment when you have to leave my sight.

On my mind you do STAY,

Promise me that you'll never go away.

To have an opportunity with you is a PLEASURE,

If given your heart, it I'll surly treasure!

At times, a word I can't even UTTER,

Overwhelmed by your charm, the heart commences to flutter,

On me, your charm has had a penetrating TOUCH,

I'm on the verge of saying I love you so much.

GOD is in the midst, I PRAY,

I'm anticipating the day, in which you'll say,

I love you too!

15

Doubt

Many claim to know what JAH is ABOUT,

Yet they still continue to suffer from doubt.

Opting to thread the road of the multitude instead of the straight and narrow ROUTE,

Most have only heard of the scriptures from the pastor or ANOTHER,

Not reading and studying for themselves, astray they continue to go further!

When one permits the mind to be SERENE,

That is when the King of King's power can permeate the scene.

Excluding or demolishing everything that threatens to wedge in BETWEEN,

Doubt's abode is truly worthy of the abyss,

Total trust in the omnipotent, don't RESIST.

One step from heaven, our earthly lives can become this.

Doubt is something to give up in a HURRY,

Sending up supplications to GOD while doubting, you should worry!

I believe it to be an offense and about the consequences, I don't want to tell that STORY!

16

Superstar

In some arena of life, everybody's a STAR,

Don't let anything here determine what you are,

From everyone else's definition, one can be FAR!

Rather it's exclusive or mainstream,

Your life is to be what you DREAM,

Choosing to command reality and disregard what things seem.

Proceeding to subdue all FEAR,

Acknowledging that your place is beyond dear,

Things you don't want, just make them DISAPPEAR.

Telling all that they are fools to doubt,

For you now tell destiny what to bring ABOUT!

There is nothing you can do but standout.

Superstar!

17

Resolution

At nothing, will I ENDEAVOR!
In my life, there is no such thing as never,
For I am the one that determine the WEATHER.
To succeed rather than try is so much better!

At nothing, will I ENDEAVOR!

Acknowledging the power in me that is divine,
My soul's divinity I'll permit nothing to UNDERMINE,
Between the hereafter and this world is a thin line.

At nothing, will I ENDEAVOR!

Anything, is what the all-knowing will grant,
Him one must learn to ENCHANT.
To believe that some good things aren't for you is a lie,
One must do and not just TRY,
Not just some, but all were meant to fly!

At nothing, will I ENDEAVOR!

To not succeed, Brahma is whom we aggrieve,
Created in his image, anything, we should be able to achieve,
To try is to doubt and to do is to BELIEVE!

18

Worry

My destiny, do I sometimes attempt to HURRY.

I must walk firmly on my track,

To worry and doubt Allah, faith is what I LACK,

Trying not to ever completely lose my way, because I may not get it back!

Wondering am I really going the right WAY,

Or with my very soul do I play!

In the grave with my father's purpose unachieved, I don't want to LAY,

So I aim to follow my heart and cease to worry on this day.

I will stop thinking so much and instead make CHOICES,

Being sensitive to GOD and my ancestors' voices.

For the approval of man and woman I don't CARE,

My GOD-bestowed individuality is what I declare!

And in this world, I will determine what is my share,

In worries habitation, action has taken up residence THERE!

19

Be yourself

In this life, one must not FOLD,

You can't please everyone I've been told.

On to your individuality, you have to HOLD,

To be ashamed of one's self is cold.

For a specific purpose, you did the Most High MOLD!

Regardless of what others think, be bold,

And happy will you wax OLD!

Be yourself

Yourself you must always DEFEND,

For someone to speak or act for you never depend.

Don't be a follower, instead dictate your own END,

To discover whom you really are, to your soul you must tend!

And with the drove refuse to BLEND!

For every person, this is an ideal trend,

Trying to be as another is what one has to TRANCEND!

20

Faith

I know just where to LOOK!

My ignorance is what GOD took!

For there is so much to be learnt in his holy BOOK,

For yourself, why don't you take a peek,

So many things will be revealed if you only SEEK!

        I know just where to LOOK!

There is no need to ask me how,

And your knees, it would be good to make them a habit to BOW,

Into your heart, JAH you should allow.

He isn't hard to FIND,

All one must do is clear their mind.

        I know just where to LOOK!

In many places does he ABIDE,

Concerning you, he needs to be on the inside!

For he's the only one in which you can CONFIDE.

        You can meet him before you die,

To believe anything else is a LIE!

To him all one have to do is send up a sincere cry,

        He will then APPEAR!

And when he does, you better hold him dear!

Now not only I, but you know just where to look also!

21

Everything has a purpose

What is it that you take LIGHT?

Nothing in JAH'S creation should we slight!

For how long will you neglect the day for the NIGHT?

To become one with GOD'S total creation we must fight.

Everything has a purpose

Indeed, everything has a REASON!

GOD fashioned everything for a particular season.

Behold the various CREATURES,

They possess such intriguing and unique features.

Being valued of JAH, they are qualified in some areas to be our TEACHERS!

A sweet melody is what most birds make,

Of there knowledge and wisdom, I aim to TAKE!

For nothing did Solomon originally forsake.

The trees, plants, ocean, and others present such a beautiful SCENE!

Can you not see GOD in between!

Everything has a purpose

Dig deep and refrain from just scratching the SURFACE,

This world is beyond being just vast,

To take nothing lightly is man's ultimate TASK!

For in the true glory of GOD'S creation can one then bask!

22

The mystery of Time

To be careful and calculate one's steps isn't a CRIME,

But, find balance because you won't always be in your prime.

Time, one must learn to NEGATE!

For you are often too early or too late,

Being right on time, some love and others HATE.

With this entity endeavor to become one,

Each moment will then be well DONE.

All you desire, you may not obtain,

Do what is important now and elude future PAIN.

One has to learn to dance in the sun and the rain!

Time, one has to learn to RESPECT,

For not one moment should you neglect,

   For your life, do time DIRECT!

Thankfulness

It is because of JAH'S grace,

That the past is gone without a TRACE!

Against me, no one has a case.

My blessings continue to MULTIPLY,

For day and night, I could testify,

His might and mercy I can't DENY.

To him I must always give homage and respect,

Aiming to be mindful because it's easy to NEGLECT,

For JAH must be recognized from every aspect!

It is healthy for one to sometimes dwell ALONE,

Letting all worldly influences be gone!

Immersing in the spirit and eluding flesh and BONE!

Render your spirit the authority to roam,

This place is temporary; it's not your HOME!

May your convictions become as solid as mine and not as foam!

24

The Sky is the Limit

Countless things may invade and threaten to HINDER,

If one press on they will eventually surrender!

Of destiny, don't become a borrower but a LENDER.

Extend your arms out and reach,

Grant the atmosphere an opportunity to TEACH,

For it's you, not the sky that commits the breach!

All is free and at your ACCESS,

Your vision, you must not touch but caress,

The sky is the limit, so settle for nothing LESS.

     Advance and keep heart,

You and your dreams are meant to be together and not APART!

     The sky being the end,

If you haven't achieved your objectives cease to PRETEND,

For look to the sky, because the earth can apprehend!

25

Provoke your Consciousness

One that peered behind the EYES,

My entire worth there it lies!

Looking on in DISBELIEF,

To my surprise, the encounter wasn't brief.

At times, I am at their complete WHIM,

With sacred drink, my cup is filled to the brim!

Disregarding what their influence might COST,

For I know that my soul won't be lost.

Being compelled by that voice that resides inside of my VOICE,

They literally control me; very rarely do I have a choice!

The shackles, I continue to TOSS,

Experiences of immortality on earth, I almost loss!

This is a sphere that's somewhat taboo and not to be expressed, but FELT,

The holy flame burns and ice around one's soul melts!

26

Otherworldly

Truly, there is no time to WORRY,

For one must become liberated and in a hurry,

Fulfilling JAH'S purpose, so another can't speculate on your STORY.

Permitting your soul to wander in space,

Realizing that you have no designated PLACE,

When the inclinations of the flesh have vanished without a trace!

Otherworldly

Attaining that sphere, in which one control TIME,

Where to be anything less than a reflection of GOD is a capital crime!

And there is no such thing as being in your PRIME,

A dimension where no one can pretend,

For everything here is so easy to COMPREHEND,

Any and everything we could mend!

This ideal reality, I hope JAH SEND.

Otherworldly

With the current world, I am out of touch,

Something I can't explain, but only feel, I constantly desire MUCH!

All I can utter is that it is of such....

Truly, there's a lot to KNOW,

Most is unimaginable things, I am convinced though!

27

Supreme Liberation

The spirit one must FREE!

From this world, you have to flee!

Reaching an area where you can look down from a distance like the bird in the TREE,

Of this wicked world, we were not meant to be.

Supreme Liberation

Anyone, JAH will REDEEM,

Live in reality and fail to only dream!

Of this world, one should have no CARE,

In the hereafter lies your true share,

Our sojourn here is so BRIEF,

Knowing that should bring a great relief,

Therefore, one must strive to do RIGHT,

For the end may be at day or night.

I implore you to seek JAH with HASTE,

For there isn't any time to waste!

This is GOD'S will,

Attain immortality and the evil you may behold and experience but not FEEL!

Different Roads

Numerous roads in life, there IS,

Find your own or another mortal may ask you to follow his.

By doing so, will you find your destiny or MISS?

It all boils down to one answer, which is this,

Follow your own soul and destiny you may just get a chance to KISS!

Different Roads

Some roads are short and others are long,

Which road is right, which road is WRONG?

My counsel is that, one asks GOD before asking another to come along,

Remember sometimes it's not what you sing but who sing's the SONG!

Different Roads

Sometimes one just has to alleviate the load,

We're spiritual beings and this flesh deteriorates, I've been TOLD!

To find your own route is worth more than any silver or gold.

Just as sure as the summer comes, ensuing is the COLD,

Perhaps we'll all be blessed to wax old,

But, in one's youth it's best to find your ROAD....

29

Never give Up

In spite of obstacles, one must PERSEVERE,
Aiming to be at the front and not the rear!
There is nothing wrong with shedding a TEAR,
That should only make one proceed in high gear.
GOD delegated you with dominion, so there's no need to FEAR,
You must achieve or possess whatever you consider dear.

Never give Up

Many troubles are inevitable and sure to EMERGE,
But, to persevere and appeal to JAH should be your urge.
Into your true destiny you will then SURGE,
You and the god inside will no doubt merge!

Never give Up

Don't ever settle for DEFEAT,
There's not a thing that you can't beat.
Make victory captive and refuse to LOSE!
To give up one must not choose,
A challenge looms to only strengthen and TRAIN,
One is bound to succeed if he maintains!

30

How do one Blend?

To her, my life, I'll DEDICATE,

But, my soul's own purpose, I must appreciate.

As one, I want us to BE,

And there have to be times only for me.

Alone, into this world, I was BROUGHT,

To love self above all must be the first lesson taught.

Various times, my soul, I did OFFEND,

Once and for all, him I set out to mend!

Licensing him to still soar while with another, I BLEND!

For truly this isn't an easy task,

To execute this, power from GOD is what I ASK,

For to grasp this mystery of divinity, one truly can bask!

To my soul, will I continue to take HEED,

Being aware that on the flesh and world my spirit can't feed.

The woman is precious, but to precede her is what my soul NEEDS,

For there is absolutely no other manner in which to blend or proceed.

31

Life

My life, do I hold in HAND,

JAH is one that I will never completely understand.

For creation is an enigma all too GRAND!

Everything, I no longer endeavor to comprehend,

And if I don't know I won't PRETEND!

But, it would be a perfect world to bring all ignorance to an end,

Life

GOD'S mercy and might will forever ENDURE,

Of this, all creation can be sure,

And humanity, he sacrificed his son FOR.

To him always dispense praise, and then make your APPEAL,

Above all, the spirit, one must pray that he keeps filled!

Realizing that everything is in vain when the spirit is deplete and STILL,

Life

Of this world, one should not think too much,

Being able to perceive beyond after experiencing JAH'S unmistakable TOUCH.

Paradise for you in every way can now begin,

Pass up the option to suffer your majesty to remain latent WITHIN!

I am Master

No one, will I allow to make my skies GRAY!

I determine what will be in my life each and every day.

Inclining my ear to those of the spiritual realm and not caring what humans SAY,

Surly, people will try to make one blue,

But, to myself, I must remain TRUE!

Those that have become god's are rare and unlike you, (the adversaries)

Of humanity's true purpose, you have no CLUE,

Yourself and reality you thought you knew.

I am Master

No one, will I allow to make my skies GRAY!

Watch what I carry out and don't just be attentive to what I say!

Everyone in the world, one can't PLEASE,

You only smother the fire when you try to appease!

I would rather have adversaries and live with my soul at EASE!

I am Master

No one, will I allow to make my skies gray!

For them, bloody tears, I do SHED!

Far from truth they have been led!

Knowing that most are only a product of what they've been BRED,

Looking into their eyes, I behold souls that are dead!

But oh no, I can't allow them to make my skies GRAY,

GOD how much longer must I witness these atrocities, not much longer I pray!

It is not what one Observes

Don't ever yield to circumstance,

With fortitude carry out your PERFORMANCE.

Because life is nothing but a big play,

And each and every person has their DAY!

But only if one listens to what JAH has to say,

It is not what one Observes

What is it that you BELIEVE?

Surly, it you can achieve.

Your own destiny is what you HOLD,

I don't care what you've been told!

The hand you've been dealt, don't you dare FOLD,

And it doesn't matter if you're young or old!

It is not what one Observes

Disregard what you SEE,

For ultimately, what matters is what you resolve to be!

GOD only said to one, "put forth effort and trust in ME."

34

Acknowledging Self

Upon the wind, do I intend to WALK,

My destiny, I will apprehend and refuse to stalk!

If I don't achieve my purpose it's my own FAULT,

Only an oaf will perpetually abide as a mortal of thought,

This battle of life, for quite sometime I've FOUGHT!

Not being the one to wish upon a star either,

Because mother destiny, clearly I can see HER.

A king I am, in pursuit of my crown!

And on me, I won't permit fate to FROWN,

For I'm the only one that can hold me down!

To everything, I do have the KEY,

Reality, JAH has blessed my eyes to see!

Infinite is the potential that's lies within ME!

35

Beware of Haste

Most choose to go forth with SPEED,

Not even including GOD in the deed!

To begin with, they're obsessed with wants and unconcerned about NEEDS,

For if one don't know JAH and self, he definitely can't succeed.

By obtaining balance one will truly be FREED,

Develop some patience before you proceed!

Beware of Haste

With forbearance, for all things in GOD we must TRUST,

To let each other down it seems as if we humans must.

If we didn't, to JAH we would never have reason to GO,

It's seems that life is short here but it takes a little time to fulfill it though.

      With care, take every TURN,

Fire purifies some and others it burn!

Beware of haste and a lot you'll LEARN.

36

Hold On

One should never cease to DREAM,

Even though quite hopeless things may seem.

For in life one will is certain to suffer and SCREAM,

But, in the end, life grants what you merit, I deem!

Plights are designed to only make one STRONG,

Something great is sure to occur when most seem wrong.

Just accept that for all good times you can't LONG,

Because you'll only end up singing a sad song!

Hold On

Life is but a short WHILE,

So even during your adversities you should try to smile.

Life is an adventure to EXPLORE,

How blessed one is to experience, and not have to ask to be told more!

To the end, you must ENDURE,

This life isn't all JAH has for us and that's for sure!

State of Mind

To be different isn't really peculiar, but UNIQUE,

Your very own gifts you have to seek!

And there's nothing wrong with being a RECLUSE,

You can be what you want and not what others choose!

Don't concur with the current view of the youth, which is, I must SHINE,

Instead, tell yourself, not everything I see can be mine!

Secure one trustworthy companion and settle DOWN,

For there are too many life-threatening epidemics going around.

It's good not to frequent a MULTITUDE,

Even better, it is to cultivate a good attitude!

What is your state of MIND?

Your own GOD-bestowed individuality you must find,

All immorality, you have to leave BEHIND.

What an ideal state of mind!

38

Reality

I must learn to bring my passions under CONTROL!

To submit to the flesh is to jeopardize the destination of the soul.

My conscience makes me aware of wrong and RIGHT,

Just as the moon knows, he is more visible during night!

The bird even knows that he's much safer during FLIGHT!

There's something otherworldly that yearns to dominate in every creature,

We have to be sensitive to this moral TEACHER!

      Mysterious though it may seem,

But, man without woman is like neglecting reality for a DREAM!

If proper knowledge dictate our actions and desires,

The soul can be assured, because it's not likely to dwell in eternal FIRE!

We should protect our hearts and minds,

Oftentimes worldly affairs and women can cause a man to be left BEHIND!

If not situated in the right perspective, we'll find ourselves in a fatal bind.

39

Smile

I want to see a smile on your FACE!

Surly, with a frown you'll lose this race.

If one is breathing, he should be RELIEVED,

For countless among us are being ushered out at a rate that is hard to believe.

And some take a smile lightly, I PERCEIVE,

In sin, it's said we humans were conceived!

Smile, for JAH was so fond of us that he gave his only SON,

His desire is that the humans become purified and one!

Smile

A sincere smile, penetrates so very DEEP!

More powerful than a spoken word and good relations it can keep,

And a smile can soothe one that WEEPS,

It can even help a neurotic one fall to sleep!

Now that I've spoken my PEACE,

Perhaps more genuine smiles will be released,

And just maybe the schism of mankind will CEASE!

40

Friends

One that will go that extra MILE,

No matter what the situation, they'll make you smile.

And their mouths is void of any GUILE!

Could there possibly be more than one golden child?

Friends

A staunch friend is one that despises SIN,

When you're wrong or upset they can make you grin.

And in all your pursuits they aim to see that you WIN!

Now this is a real friend,

Their loyalty outshines that of one that is KIN!

Morals is what they desire, if they don't already possess,

And folly is something they utterly DETEST!

I would reconcile for nothing less,

For a friend of this quality is the BEST!

In their presence, you'll truly find rest.

41

Metamorphosis

This isn't merely a casual CHANGE!

It's a supernatural event and surpasses being just strange,

Your entire life, it will sometimes utterly REARRANGE.

This happens be an unusual transition,

Which hands over to one a new VISION.

Supreme power is found in effort accompanied by sincere supplication,

To undergo such an experience, is a GOD- sent REVEALATION!

And this should be the most sought after emancipation,

Metamorphosis

Such an occurrence goes beyond what most earthlings BELIEVE,

It's not for us to wholly understand, so be relieved,

There are inhuman influences, so cooperate and your mission will be ACHIEVED.

By resolution, we will be granted aid to transform into what our hearts conceive!

42

Confrontation 2

To me, a challenge, did life PROPOSE!

For to partake of this adventure, I gladly chose,

From deep within my soul, is where acceptance AROSE,

The one's intimidated by life, I can't come to reflect those!

Realizing I must keep the door ajar and not CLOSED,

To be led by JAH is to really be alive,

Having balance and knowing when to be still and when to DRIVE,

At times, we have to know when to strive,

But, in some cases we must wait patiently for it to ARRIVE!

Life has a script for us all to play,

Embark on the journey and accomplish something EVERYDAY.

In the end, you hold the might to define,

For the challenge of life is always imminent and seeks a chance to UNDERMINE,

But, your immortal soul can leap beyond life here, so it, you better enshrine!

Aspirations

Effort has to be the forerunner of hope it SEEMS!

This is the only way in which one can bring to reality a dream,

Aspirations are so intimate with matter I DEEM!

For this is what I oftentimes witness my soul scream.

It can definitely be done again if it's been done BEFORE,

All your life, another don't adore,

Your dreams proceed to CHASE,

For you weren't necessarily assigned a designated place!

Aspirations

Cease to wish on a STAR,

In control of your fate, you are!

And from JAH, you must not be FAR,

Created in GOD'S mighty image, are you!

Dreams are realities awaiting transformation, now that's TRUE.

Anxious for one to clutch it's hand and say I do,

In some instances, she only grants one opportunity, and not TWO,

Aspirations should no longer be gray but blue!

CHAPTER 3

Divine and Frame of Mind!

That that is sacred can only be seen by those that possess discipline and are divinely inclined. The true and faithful spiritual aspirant is usually left to thread this road less traveled alone. The external world becomes mediocre and a mystery worth indulging in. Consequently, their lives eventually become their story! It commences to speak volumes, and sometimes these volumes are unearthly. Just to be in their presence or behold them in society is a blessing, and this happening awards the viewer or viewers with more wisdom that could ever fall from the uncommon one's lips! However, one must be sensitive and receptive to the light when it shines. Some of these individuals opt not to utter much because they know that mortals absorb more from what they see than what they hear. In the event of being aware of this, the messiahs choose to demonstrate by action, and yes, I said messiahs, because the term can take on various meanings, and messiahs can have different missions or callings.

Nevertheless, one's frame of mind sometimes will change just as the weather. I counsel you to ask GOD to bless you to know the seasons, because there is a time for everything under the sun. Only then will one know what frame of mind to employ. To achieve this, is to truly enter the ranks of the noble and the paradise bound!

Divine and Frame of Mind!

1

Testament

For the world, I have one great STORY,

Do any really know how it feels to be consumed by JAH'S glory?

Instead of trusting in him, many go through life and WORRY.

Not knowing that without trust, numerous blessings, away they hurry,

Testament

We must learn to dispel STRESS,

And at GOD'S faithfulness to us, we should never guess!

Because JAH'S presence is everything trying to encourage mankind to CONFESS,

That without him, we all do settle for less.

If one seek, upon your soul, holiness he will IMPRESS!

2

Optimism

Over life, I refuse to FRET,

What one put into life is what he gets!

For I haven't seen anything that I believe I can't have YET!

To life, one usually has to pay a debt,

It'll be facilitated, if into your heart JAH you LET.

Over life, I refuse to FRET,

Without GOD, you'll never live the best and on that I'll bet.

On the Most High cast your every WORRY,

And learn to be patient and not always in a hurry!

For in time, you may come to possess a great STORY.

Over life, I refuse to FRET!

Your life can be fulfilled from every aspect,

But, you have to love JAH first and show yourself RESPECT.

And others humans, be careful not to neglect,

For GOD'S image we all can truly one day REFLECT!

To fret one must refuse,

Take action and pray and you won't LOSE!

3

Just be Thankful

You may not have a great big HOUSE,

For one may not even have a faithful spouse!

You may not even have a roof over your HEAD,

Perhaps you have even come to know the ground as your bed,

But, you still have a chance because you're among the living and not the DEAD!

Just be Thankful

To better your condition, you must pray and STRIVE,

If you give up, you may as well be dead than alive!

GOD still loves you and any other notion is sheer JIVE!

One is certain to get a breakthrough, if he keeps a positive drive.

Just be Thankful

The house with several rooms and exotic ART,

The wife that's not only faithful but smart!

Most of your family members are still HERE,

Your very presence, convicts people, and you, some fear!

Just be Thankful

To better your condition you must STRIVE,

If you give up, you may as well be dead than alive!

GOD still loves you and any other notion is sheer JIVE!

4

Praise

Reverence for Jehovah is never out of season,

Every time we draw a breath, Jesus is the REASON!

Mankind was created to magnify his name,

By neglecting this duty, one becomes destined for eternal SHAME!

The compassion JAH holds goes beyond human understanding,

Granting us free will, for he is never DEMANDING.

Praise GOD! Praise GOD, those that have activity of their members!

Grievous it would be, if Emmanuel had not descended from heaven in DECEMBER,

Praise for the almighty must always be shown and remembered.

5

Deliberation

JAH bless me with an eagle's WINGS,
So, I can rise above the storm that life brings!
For one is likely to suffer so many bad THINGS,
Oftentimes, I have no idea of which way to step,
For so very long has my soul WEPT.
But, my trust in you, I have kept!

Deliberation

When will my circumstances CHANGE?
A lot of troubles sometime come to those that do good, how strange,
What is it, that my soul really SEEK?
At my true destiny, I'll say I desire to peek,
Me, do life, sometimes CONFUSE,
Yet myself, I will not let anyone abuse!
My end will truly be just what I CHOOSE,
And there isn't possibly a way that I'll lose,

For I have paid my DUES!

6

GOD'S Mercy

This is something that one cannot EARN,

From your iniquity just endeavor to turn.

Usually on your own, you won't succeed at THIS,

Without crying out to GOD, your attempt is wholly amiss!

When I decided to truly REPENT,

A new sense of being is what JAH sent.

And this was one mysterious EVENT,

Out the window, my old being truly went!

At first, I tried to change by myself, and all ALONE,

Without succeeding, my soul continued to suffer and moan.

Then I declared that totally in GOD, I would DEPEND,

And my fervent prayer and effort brought about change, I still don't comprehend!

One must become acquainted with the one I praise and RESPECT,

The belief that you can do something alone, you have to reject!

7

Good and Evil

I envision good and evil being torn ASUNDER,

Just as the sky is pierced by the thunder!

For anyone to delight in immorality could be a fatal BLUNDER,

JAH'S ten commandment's, humanity is suppose to obey and abide under.

How much longer will mortals bask in sin, I WONDER?

Good and Evil

Most are overwhelmed by GREED,

And acts of self-concern is their primary deed,

On righteousness, one should aim to feed.

Evil must not be permitted to spring forth, so eradicate the SEEDS!

We are able to triumph over evil's events,

There is supreme power in good, because it's GOD-SENT!

8

Take a Look

Daily at your life, take a LOOK,

The course one travel must be straight and lacking any crooks!

The highest knowledge pours from within, transcending every BOOK!

Prior to discovering this, knowledge from everybody else I took,

When I begun to seek JAH, my soul he SHOOK!

Take a Look

What is it that you would like to know?

For true knowledge comes from above and not on earth BELOW!

On your life, allow GOD to blow,

Don't believe you can't experience heavenly bliss here because another said SO.

The god in you yearns to awake,

Permit him to be free for your soul's SAKE!

For this life is fleeting and in contrast to the afterworld its fake,

To live a lie or live the truth, which choice will you MAKE?

Not to accept your majesty is the greatest mistake.

9

Burdens

It's difficult sometimes to see beyond my CARES,

So many concerns seem threatening to my welfare!

And at times, it seems as if Yahweh isn't THERE,

I'm really wondering how much more of this I can bear!

Beginning to think that for some, life just isn't FAIR,

But, to give up, myself do I dare!

Will I become engulfed by the PAIN?

Every time I try to move forward, backwards two steps, I gain!

No longer do I wonder why many people go INSANE.

And nobody can I attribute with the blame,

The maker and I are responsible for all in my life that has CAME,

After undergoing such pain, one will definitely not be the same!

You will either be strengthened or destroyed by the FLAME,

I've heard some utter that life is one deadly game!

Burdens

My heart must cease to FRET,

These eyes, I hate to see red and wet.

Therefore, cold I think I should GET!

My good times haven't started to outweigh my bad ones yet!

And it may never be that way, I'm willing to BET,

But, in despair I will not sit!

And to dear struggle, do I tilt my HAT,

Believing me to forever be part of it!

10

The Fight

Life happens to be one unpredictable DRAMA,

Sometimes making one wish, he never had a dad or mama!

Why was I even BORN?

More affliction than happiness I've worn,

For some answers about the mystery of life, I MOURN,

Knowing that my time here is a brief sojourn.

Opting not to pick the oppressor's CORN!

And from reality, I'll never again be torn,

Anticipating that day in which I'll hear that heavenly HORN.

The Fight

For truth and understanding I yearn,

But, for refusing simplicity, will I BURN?

It's so many things to be experienced here on earth,

At times, it makes one curse his very BIRTH!

For the truth, to GOD we must look,

Hoping for a personal encounter, so we don't have to open the BOOK!

Out of life, I resolve to get the most,

Of my enlightenment and achievements, I'll never BOAST.

Recognizing that it's not me, but JAH, and some call him the holy GHOST!

The Fight

What the omnipotent grant, one has to ESTEEM,

If it doesn't appear good to the mortal eye, why me one usually scream!

GOD is a respecter of persons, do it sometimes SEEM,

But I think those given the greatest mission, he pursues hard,

Strengthening them by countless trials, so Satan can't easily BOMBARD!

11

Zion

The righteous is who the world MOCK,

On Zion's door, I am ready to knock!

There aren't many left of JAH'S chosen FLOCK,

On the majority of the world, the door is sure to lock!

Dreadful it will be not to make it IN,

Opting to reject righteous for pleasure and sin!

This holy race is one in which only a few will WIN.

Zion

These troubles, we have to weather,

In Zion the sinner and the righteous won't dwell TOGETHER,

To live among Yahweh and his host what could possibly be better!

From his grace, so many have FELL,

On the next world, they don't care think or dwell.

The door is truly AJAR,

For those that seek to be close and not afar!

Take action and no longer wish on the STAR,

A powerful godly being is who you are!

And in Zion is where you BELONG,

To subsist in an ungodly manner is wrong.

Only the LORD of LORDS can make one STRONG,

For Zion, I so passionately long!

12

JAH control

Render JAH your SOUL,

For Satan aims to destroy when he's in control!

That divine flame one can IGNITE,

And for mortal perfection, we must fight,

For JAH, this notion really does EXCITE!

To accept morality, is the way to abide,

Satan is hard to get rid of when he gets on the INSIDE!

Anything is possible when GOD has been put first,

One must not only desire, but also THIRST!

From evil he will deliver,

Moving about like a flame on the inside, causing one not to SHIVER!

The soul, he will do more than satisfy,

Your thirst and effort causes him to MAGNIFY.

To most, you become quite strange,

Many will never experience such a CHANGE,

Render him utter control,

For infinite will become the power of your SOUL!

13

The greatest Thrill

A spiritual destiny, we all have to FULFILL!

Sometimes it can't be seen but it's so real,

Your thoughts possess the potential to protect or make ILL.

For dormant lies your spiritual will,

This world is material, carnal, and constantly intending to KILL.

The greatest Thrill

Things are fleeting in this world, and me, it sometimes annoy,

For pleasure is all most want to ENJOY,

And wisdom is something they are determined not to employ.

This is what I ultimately REALIZED,

To obtain access to the hereafter from earth is to be civilized!

This sphere isn't difficult to reach, but it is hard, if not impossible to STAY,

Your love and obsession for the world, to waste, it you must lay,

For the greatest thrill, this is the price one has to PAY!

14

Life's Mystery

Do you know what you are to do, for sure?

At least peer, if you don't go and investigate what's behind every DOOR,

How can one be sure of his or her way without being exposed before?

From this journey, a great number take a detour!

But, life will soon or later utter that it's best to face me now than IGNORE.

Life's Mystery

By great throngs they remain behind,

Instead of emancipating destiny, him they permit life to BIND!

To the truth seeker, the immortals are usually kind,

How unfortunate it is that the answer to the riddle of life, here we won't ever

completely FIND!

15

GOD Lives

To the lost, redemption is what he gives!

He manifests his self in various WAYS,

In one image he never stays.

Exceedingly powerful and lively is HE,

And in every persons life, is where Brahma was meant to be.

Without him, one can't accomplish the MOST,

He even sends to your aid the heavenly host!

To JAH, we mortals must yield a TOAST!

GOD Lives

He can be seen in every creature,

For nothing in creation lacks his FEATURES.

His majesty, we will never fathom,

Words acknowledging that our father lives should become the world's

ANTHEM!

Never will he lead us astray,

Look at creation and GOD lives one must SAY!

Only a fool would deny this today,

Allah lives and is willing to lead us in the holy way.

16

Ascend

Will such great masses really continue to SLEEP?
On earth, paradise you can't really behold, but you can get a peep,
Life is a phenomenon and the soul is too DEEP!
Assured am I, but for others, I weep,
My soul is not the only one I desire the LORD to KEEP!

Ascend

When you suffer, so do I,
Come with me and find your place in the sky.
When one with GOD, beyond this world you LIE,
Most have chosen to experience perdition twice and I want to know why!
They don't realize that the world's on fire and the body must DIE,
And that the spirit is destined to either burn or fly!
On that day of reckoning, to you, I'll hate to say GOODBYE!

Ascend

Nearer than you realize has become that DAY,
While there is still time one must pray.
The soul is holy, so rebuke what the flesh SAY,
We were originally fashioned to live in a pure way.

Woe to him who's work is undone when up is his STAY!

At peace with the spirit, I pray you be,

In a short while JAH'S countenance we are going to SEE!

17

Contentment

The master, one cannot CONFINE,

The glory is his and not mine!

As a light, he caused me to SHINE!

The feeling is something, I can't explain,

Only for myself, nothing do I seek to OBTAIN,

Souls for GOD, is what I hope to gain!

Contentment

And about nothing, do I WORRY,

At peace am I, and following the maker in a hurry.

To share with the world, he has given me a great STORY!

It was Lucifer and I, until the almighty came between,

The power I felt and the light I SEEN!

In faith and sincerity only, must one act,

Those otherworldly beings, this does ATTRACT!

To abide in contentment brings the supreme thrill,

Only a few find their purpose and this life they FULFILL!

18

As you believe, so you Are

In truth, you are nothing short of GRAND,

To be wrought in GOD'S image, this do you understand.

For that that one believes, will definitely be in his HAND,

First, it's called forth from the spiritual realm then on land.

As you believe, so you Are

One must be pliant to the soul's URGE,

Of all immorality, yourself you have to purge,

This is the only way in which your true destiny can SURGE.

Some choose to reflect Lucifer's face,

To be different from the world to them is out of PLACE.

Instead of reality, a fantasy, they would rather chase!

As you believe, so you Are

In your divinity, please BELIEVE,

For Satan is always on the prowl trying to deceive!

Why not just open your eyes and PERCEIVE,

That one is only the product of what he believes!

19

Spiritual Brother

The brother most never HAD!

For you my heart is so very glad.

The majority never get this, how SAD.

Never have I ever experienced anything like this,

By not consulting JAH, numerous blessing people MISS!

Now destined for heaven, but at one time we both inhabited the abyss!

Spiritual Brother

The brother most never HAD!

When we're together GOD loves to intervene,

Uttering by the fire of these two souls, my great light can indeed be SEEN!

Us, I ask him to never let anything wedge between.

To you, I will always give honor and RESPECT,

From the very first day, our souls did connect!

I envision a life-long BROTHER-HOOD,

If there's anything I can ever do for you I would.

The impossible we can achieve, I really believe we COULD!

20

Exile

To truly ferret out who you are, resort to EXILE,

Allow the spirit to forever dominate or at least for a little while.

Indeed, you, the world seek to DEFILE.

And what causes pain may eventually bring a smile!

Remove far from the MULTITUDE,

Communion with one's self is detrimental to elude,

Only those that's not of this dimension, INCLUDE!

Exile

With haste, proceed to JAH'S throne,

In the world, most mortals suffer from fear of being ALONE,

What a noble feeling it must be when the influences of the flesh are gone!

And GOD'S spirit can truly speak and cease to moan!

On this path is so very FEW,

Because from the world they withdrew.

Realizing that they could somewhat experience the hereafter on earth TO!

No longer do they ask, I am who,

To the potter's plan, they've said I DO,

Having accepted their godliness, unlike you!

A glimpse of the plan, I SAW,

Invincible is the spirit, and from it, there's nothing one can't draw!

Almost every moment for me now, is like a state of AWE.

21

Despair

This heavy load would anyone be sympathetic to SHARE!

I'm beginning to wonder if GOD is really there,

He promised he would put no more on me than I could BARE!

Oh, if I had the wings of an eagle, I would take to the air!

First unloading my every CARE,

Oh, father, my lament, I wonder if you hear.

Despair

The anguish I'm going through is too PROFOUND!

For a mental impairment, I pray I'm not bound,

My soul has begun to make an unworldly sound!

And my head is spinning around and around,

I must stay on my feet and off the GROUND.

Even though me, oh grim despair continue to pound!

In defeat, I refuse to be FOUND!

Despair

When this occurs, I disappear where,

I can gather my thoughts and consider asking GOD if he's being FAIR.

To question him, myself should I dare?

Even in the event of DESPAIR!

I'm convinced that JAH is always there,

But, sometimes the heavy load causes a great SCARE.

Therefore, everyone must prepare,

For the inevitable battle with oh grim DESPAIR!

The Shadow

The entity that only emerges at NIGHT,

Often mistaken for a second person and causes a great fright.

For his image does TRANSFORM,

A good purpose I believe he has, so turn off the alarm.

Mysterious, will he REMAIN,

A futile existence he surly doesn't retain!

Simply because GOD doesn't make anything in VAIN!

The Shadow

This is our companion in the darkness,

Perhaps he was sent to protect the good from the HEARTLESS.

At the sight of dawn, he does vamoose,

Abruptly all association with us is cut loose.

Perhaps what we're inclined to miss he is there to SEE,

Being of the darkness, but also connected to you and me!

Little value, we often designate as his LOT,

Who knows, without him at night, could be a fatal blot!

Deception

Many people thrive on playing GAMES!
If you take part and lose, you are to blame,
When deceived, one's heart is likely to burn like a FLAME.
Mankind is full of beast and they decline to be tamed!

Deception

Why won't they just play by the RULES?
What goes around, comes back around, you fools,
To desire the prestige of a deceiver is so UNCOOL.
These manner of individuals must be thoroughly schooled!
Only temporary will a liar be SOOTHED.

Deception

Don't have an inclination to lead people astray,
For a laugh, some will ruin another's DAY.
The game of deceit is such a deadly game to play,
Be aboveboard and falsehood don't PORTRAY!

What's Next?

Sometimes I take things out of context,
My spirits, life oftentimes VEX,
And I'm one that's not addicted to sex!
Life is constantly in MOTION,
What's next, do anyone have the slightest notion?

What's Next?

If it's not felt in the heart, don't let it PERSUADE,
Ask GOD and his army to give aid.
No matter what happens, petitions to him must be MADE,
We don't always know the season,
But, everything occurs for a REASON.
In spite of anything, you have to strive,
If you give up, you might as well not even be ALIVE!

What's Next

What ever comes about, you are to truly blame,

For when you dictate, things can't remain the SAME.

Especially when gratifying Yahweh is one's aim,

You were delegated with power to righteously COMMAND,

And everything in life, you will never understand.

But, to be wrought in the likeness of JEHOVAH renders you GRAND,

Regardless of what's next, destiny is always in your hand!

25

I am not Alone

Me, did someone DEPRIVE!

Accepting that, by myself, at my mission's end, I can't arrive,

For to be alone is nothing but mere JIVE.

Every invisible influence isn't good to reject,

You are constantly bombarded by a seen or unseen AFFECT.

At times, I drift far off into this zone,

In which a deeper self emerges and is KNOWN!

Someone else becomes present and this world is gone,

There is supernatural liberation in being ALONE!

Usually this is when that great light is turned on,

The one that causes the soul to MOAN,

Without such influences, one would surly, be evil prone!

I am not Alone

Who is it really that leaves the IMPRESSION?

From every event in life, there is a lesson,

Alone, one won't make it far is my CONFESSION.

To neglect these encounters could be the greatest transgression!

You just can't abide alone HERE,

Rather your influences remain unseen or appear.

26

Man, why are you afraid to Cry?

Just give me one good reason why?

To say that it is unmanly is a LIE.

GOD designed this emotion to flow,

And not only when one is feeling LOW.

Sometimes the tears come fast and at other times they come slow,

It takes a real man to cry THOUGH!

Man, why are you afraid to Cry?

Until you release every faculty, you can't fly,

One must know this truth before he DIES.

The belief that only woman can engage in this emotion, don't buy,

If you don't believe me, look for the truth in the SKY.

Man's foolish belief concerning this, makes me blue,

The truth about this matter he doesn't really have a CLUE.

So LORD, what am I to do?

But, pray and hope that man recognizes the power of tears before this life is

THROUGH!

Pain and Pleasure

Sometimes one don't know what he's feeling,

But, sinister are humans who feel pleasure when KILLING.

To help a person in need should always be a pleasure,

Some people see it as a pain to share their earthly TREASURES.

Most are fond of fornication, and say that the heat usually gets intense,

From an unearthly standpoint, this isn't right or makes much SENSE.

Perform a thorough examination of your brain,

What is it that you are experiencing, pleasure or pain.

Sometimes, endeavoring to distinguish between the two, threatens to drive one insane,

They run so very close together that I've decided to call them sunshine and RAIN!

28

The Mind: part 1

Too much thinking can be of great HARM,

Balanced thought and action takes on GOD-like form!

Concentration on one matter at a time should be INTENSE,

To overwhelm the mind causes one to fail and is non-sense.

Never allow the mind to FRET,

An order for balanced thought and action you must set,

And into the mind, JAH one surly have to LET.

The Mind: part 1

When fully developed and trained, this is what you'll find,

None other then the infinity and all-conquering power of the MIND!

This causes one to be free and able to remain,

No matter what the world inflicts rather, it is joy or PAIN.

Always hope and aim for the best,

For in the hereafter, the conscious will truly be awarded REST.

And don't only desire material gain,

Spiritual and mental wealth is the only thing that really must be OBTAINED!

With the mind, don't take a chance,

By the feeding of proper knowledge, beyond your imagination, it will ADVANCE!

29

The Tread among the Dead

Spiritual riches, they don't care to obtain!

If it doesn't pacify the flesh they say it's INSANE,

Father, why do they neglect the sun for the rain?

This walk among the dead brings unbearable PAIN!

By the world, they permit their precious spirits to be slain.

The Tread among the Dead

In despair and everlasting fantasy seems to be their LOT,

To attain mortal perfection they won't give a little, much less all they got.

In the moment some delight, and for pleasure others LIVE,

Unfortunately, this kind won't ever have much in any way to give.

Some days I suffer tremendous SORROW,

Not today, but peradventure they'll awaken tomorrow!

I resolve to give in every way and not let one BORROW.

The Tread among the Dead

Lonely it gets at times, I've heard this SAID,

But, one must try to lead and not be led.

And how can you walk straight if always down is your HEAD,

For so mysterious is this tread,

Please don't stop, but continue to walk among the DEAD!

30

Spiritual Freedom

When one no longer needs external SUPPORT,

Oh, what joy it is when the material and physical you abort!

Having been freed of having to SORT...

      Transient, usually is your stay,

Wishing you could live forever in this WAY,

Maybe in the next world you can, if here, you work hard night and day!

Sometimes it is easy to reach this SPHERE,

But, who can abide there or stay near?

Spiritual Freedom

One just can't afford to look BACK,

For if you aren't killed, surly they are dying to attack.

But, you must still stay firm on the less traveled TRACK,

Oh, when one no longer needs external support,

What joy it is when the material and physical you ABORT.

31

The Mind: part 2

The mind is the greatest human DEVICE!

Try to avoid making the same mistake twice.

What is it that you think you DESERVE?

Most are ignorant of self and gone are their nerves!

The soul does one curse and not BLESS,

Doubting the mind and causing needless stress.

To reality, you must no longer be BLIND,

Instead, exercise the potential of your mind.

In this world, go forth and get your SHARE,

To be all you can be, most don't care.

32

Apprehend Solitude

The benefits of solitude, do I apprehend,

No other physical presence to influence the message my soul SENDS.

During this occurrence, I do not have to pretend,

      For I alone set the TREND,

My disconnected or broken pieces, the creator, and I mend.

Everything that is of no avail, I REND,

Realizing that only on the maker and myself ,can I depend,

Needing no mortal help, because for myself, I can FEND.

Apprehend Solitude

You were fashioned individually, and not in a multitude,

Therefore, one will discover his uniqueness only in SOLITUDE.

Fear of self and aloneness causes one to go contrary, I have to conclude,

A reasonable passion for seclusion must dominate your ATTITUDE.

Countless blessings issue from apprehending solitude!

Introduction

CHAPTER 4

Rebellion and Unrest !

As long as there is oppression, injustice, racism, and neglect, there will always be rebellion and unrest!

The unjust practices against the Afrikan continues and must be exposed. For the havoc, that America perpetrates is so unbearable that it would be a crime against my people living and definitely against those that have physically expired if I was to be reticent. However, these practices exist abroad as well, especially in America and my homeland, Afrika.

Rebellion!

For we built America and other places as well! The land of various regions and continents are stained with our sweat and blood! For our contributions and labor is beyond measure. Our cry must be heard and our fight escalated!

Unrest!

For I can't rest because the evil is so prevalent and inhumane! Indeed they are audacious, uncaring, and worthy of perdition!

Just for the record, those grim and deceitful mortals of the European race know who they are. I do not condemn all of you. Sadly it is the majority of you though.

Their sins ascended to the heavens a long time ago! Now, I await the day of reckoning so impatiently! The day in which the blood on their hands is brought to the light. Some of their descendants will have to answer for carrying their legacy on. Countless of them continue to benefit, and not try to set the record straight!

True apology and Reparations are long overdue! The true emancipation of Afrika is too!

Rebellion and bloody Unrest!

Rebellion and Unrest !

1

African Dignity: part 2

On me, the ex-slave master continue to try and heap DISGRACE,

To no avail because I've discovered the royalty of my race.

Accepting the fact that I have to abandon this PLACE,

Resolving to orchestrate a master plan that will succeed by GOD'S grace!

No matter what evil the oppressor comes with, it I will FACE,

One usually utters, aim for the stars, but I now aim for deep space,

All because of Afrika's unsurpassed history that I TRACED!

African Dignity: part 2

They can't do anything to hinder this plan,

JAH is in the midst, and he is more powerful than MAN.

For the sake of the ancient one's, to the Europeans, I'll make my demand,

And in true unity, it is time for all Afrikans to stand.

Crying out to GOD and the ancestors to take my HAND,

And lead my people from this dreadful land!

African Dignity: part 2

I demand unlimited liberty and nothing LESS,

And I will resort to any means necessary, I must confess.

A fighter of wickedness, my soul the maker will truly BLESS,

My life do I yield entirely to this cause, I will profess,

And there is no other woman than my Afrikan queen I would CARESS!

Inspired by: Bob Marley

2

Progress

Why can't we all just PROGRESS?

Only one who lacks confidence will oppress!

Some choose to keep others from getting AHEAD,

Then to grant justice they would rather see them dead.

Ourselves we do have an obligation to DEFEND,

Do for ourselves or as last our entire lives we'll spend.

      What is the greatest SIN?

Maybe it's when a people refuse to fight evil until they win!

      To us, there is nothing NEW,

Love our enemies and hate ourselves is a philosophy we must undo.

Is there anything we haven't SEEN?

We are the chosen and between Yahweh and us, nobody can come between.

In dedication to black Martyrs: Malcolm X, Huey P. Newton, Marcus Garvey and many others!

3

Black Pride

From my true essence, I will not HIDE!

Their plans of havoc are still wide,

      In JAH'S hands, I do RESIDE.

And with the greatest ills, did I collide,

Literally taking the oppressors dictates as my BRIDE!

Laboring and ensuring his welfare, in me he once could confide,

But now, I am resolute to bring back Afrika's ancient STRIDE.

      And Revenge, I will try to put aside,

Realizing that the oppressor's heart must have really DIED.

Black Pride

About my true legacy they did lie,

Then they turned around and gave me the evil EYE!

But, a people with such a deep soul, JAH heard our cry,

Afrika's unparalleled achievements suffice more than enough for a spiritual HIGH.

America came with all the evil she had and I or the natives didn't die,

I will no longer be exploited or abused no matter how hard they TRY.

4

In the Night

They would rather attack me in the night than the DAY,

Thinking at that time, I would be easy prey.

But, GOD protects me at all times as I go on about my WAY,

For if they kill me I will influence another and still make them pay!

Some of my very own people the ex-slave master EMPLOY,

Having them to believe that money is the supreme joy.

Not knowing reality or their true identity, they quickly AGREE,

To help the evil one discredit or assassinate people like me!

The conspiracy is usually executed in the NIGHT,

Choosing to work through ignorant blacks and stay out of sight.

Because they have no courage for a man to man FIGHT!

It may even be in the day sometimes when they strike, but they are still hid,

On their involvement, do they try to keep a LID.

Wanting to remain in the dark and cover up what they did,

Of the earth, these kinds of people, GOD will rid!

5

Silence Speaks

Most of the time I am silent to permit my appearance and actions to SPEAK,

Because of this some silly mortals mistaken me for being weak.

But, true wisdom it is evident to see that they don't SEEK,

Due to ignorance, at the truth, they can't even peak!

My very spirit utters who I am ALOUD,

Delighting in the presence of my ancestors and GOD, avoiding the human crowd.

Basking in the event of putting my head in the CLOUDS,

Some may esteem me as being too proud.

But, if I am, to our father do I have to ATONE,

This mystical path, I travel alone.

The dawn of reality is here and it is time for all lies to be GONE,

If one desires to know the truth, it can now be known!

Don't look on me as being STRANGE,

Not being of the world so don't ever expect me to change.

Now you may be wondering just who is this FELLO,

To this conscious one, you are reluctant to utter a compassionate hello,

Knowing it is darkness that moves you, I remain MELLO.

6

Fire at Full Blaze

It is at full blaze INDEED,

Circumventing and sparing those few true creeds.

Causing the heart of the wicked to BLEED,

And the righteous, on the fire they must feed.

Because into the Promised Land is where I lead,

Being commissioned with authority from his MAJESTY.

The Anglo Saxon must suffer the wrath of the almighty,

Because his chosen will soon defy all forms of CAPTIVITY.

It is at full blaze INDEED,

Circumventing and sparing those few true creeds.

And the sinners can not FLEE,

For centuries, you brutalized me!

Fear is what I've begun to SEE,

And JAH says retribution is what it will surly be.

Because your morality is what you gave up, for FREE,

And your sins are too vast to be forgiven and casted into the sea.

It is at full blaze INDEED,

Circumventing and sparing those few true creeds.

Consuming everyone and everything that's of an evil SEED,

To combat Satan spiritually or incarnate is the greatest deed.

And the truth will soon be here for the world to SEE,

A repeating of the black man's superior history!

For we were the first son's of his MAJESTY,

Come close and feel the mighty fire burning inside of me!

7

Plot against the Black Revolutionary

They are heavily on my TRACKS,

Because I've discovered that we are regal blacks.

The works of JAH do they ATTACK,

But, until my demise, I will fight back!

(He is a threat, due to the way he ACTS,

If he influences others, we may lose our dominance and that's a fact!)

Plot against the Black Revolutionary

They are afraid of what we may SCORE,

But, their blood I don't care to see pour.

I just want to go back Afrika and watch the birds of Eden SOAR,

And be treated as a man and nothing more,

Now is this really to much to ask FOR?

This will become a reality rather by peace or war,

A revolutionary that's determined to see his people walk through freedom's DOOR!

8

The Load

When one obtains knowledge, he usually makes a SACRIFICE,

The discovery of things often comes with a price.

It is similar to rolling loaded DICE,

A piece of obligations pie does one slice.

Life is subject to be painful and not too NICE,

You have a duty to contend against those that are cold as ice.

But, you have the power to transform these men into MICE,

One must take away their sugar and impose on them spice.

The Load

This is power that you often take the liberty to put in your HAND,

It will cause you to forever wear a brand.

What it is that you don't UNDERSTAND,

Is that knowledge brings one duties and pain, but also makes one grand,

Knowing why the ills are and how to eradicate them from this LAND!

9

War

Every since they raped Africa, her descendants have wore a SCAR,

My ancestors' enslavers eventually defined who they are.

Our original hue was once so black and beautiful and of TAR,

Now as the lion some of us do roar,

Being told that from the creator we were FAR,

War

I, for one, just can't seem to rest!

People of such royal ancestry did they INFEST!

Now the European thinks of all GOD'S people, he is the best!

War

I know that we are the most blessed PEOPLE,

But, you treat us not as an equal!

Africa, we will FREE,

In mental or physical captivity, no more blacks will be!

And in Africa, all my people will DWELL,

Any one else's efforts of occupying the Motherland will fail!

The tables must turn, can't you TELL,

And until that day my soul won't be WELL,

The oppressor is going to burn in hell!

10

Going Wrong

Are we really going wrong?
No, we have only become mentally STRONG!
And for true liberty, we won't long.

Going Wrong

How do you know that your way is RIGHT?
For it has not yet led us into the light,
Tradition is something, I continue to SLIGHT.
Independence of thought is the greatest tool,
Renouncing old beliefs and beginning to search instead of remaining a FOOL!

Going Wrong

Could this be the season?
Is it time to wreak TREASON?
For the African has countless reasons!
Deranged, am I declared to be, when contrary to popular THOUGHT,
From another continent, I was unwillingly brought!
And the black man's redemption by any means necessary must be SOUGHT,
For my people I am sold out and can't be bought!

Going Wrong

Your path brothers and sisters, isn't RIGHT!

To alter your path, I'll endeavor with all my might,

My people must see the LIGHT!

I will not be taken out of the race,

And if I have to, I'll double my PACE!

For so long we have been a living disgrace,

Our adversary lies out a plan and we abide by it and TRACE.

Now you must prepare to go right!

And bask in JAH'S beautiful LIGHT!

11

Not as the Masses

Still can't see yet many have glasses!
On their brains the white man continue to inflict LASHES,
With this man, the enlightened Afrikan suffer deadly clashes.
My people he constantly DEPRIVES,
Mentally and spiritually, they are not alive,
In the light of truth, will they ever ARRIVE?

Not as the Masses

Alone, I may just have to go,
Because as the masses, I refuse to be SO,
Delighting in darkness and about the truth, they don't care to know!
To traditions and clichés they ADHERE,
Of not being as the crowd, most fear,
Choosing to look through a dirty glass, instead of wiping it CLEAR!

Not as the Masses

It's sad to see them sat in their ways,
Most of their knowledge being carried over from the slavery DAYS!
Opting to accept the cold of winter instead of the sun's rays,
In captivity is where their souls may STAY.

12

Being proud of your Hue

For indeed some are darker than BLUE,

Incorporated in our group are brown, yellow, red, and others too!

Of Africa, nothing most KNEW,

However, today everything is almost right in front of you.

Your roots are deep and in the past, the enslavers tried to determine how they GREW!

Being proud of your Hue

Some act ashamed and just don't know what to do,

Their ability to think and question, the world SLEW.

How sometimes I wish I was darker than blue,

And perhaps on countless other sources in Africa, I could've DREW.

And between my flesh and soul the wind could've blew,

Both would be in constant harmony maybe because of my original HUE!

Inspired by: Curtis Mayfield

13

Youth's Plight

I aim to dismantle the oppressor's plan with all my MIGHT,

Even willing to sacrifice my life for this fight.

For the black youth's future isn't BRIGHT,

And to the forthcoming revolution, I hold on tight.

Hoping that the youth will eventually see the LIGHT,

Awareness of their ancestry erects them to full height.

But right now illusion and mis-education is dimming their SIGHT

Through sports and entertainment the American pie, they try to bite!

To exchange one's soul for materialistic things isn't RIGHT,

Money usually brings about many issues and causes death or a great fright.

To the truth, they are BLIND,

But, I hope GOD forbid them to be left behind.

I have to get inside of their MINDS!

And remove the doctrines that bind,

The past is what I have to REWIND.

The only way to better their condition,

Is to assume a revolutionary POSITION!

14

Immortality

Surly, those that are conscious knows that he's still HERE,

When listening to his emancipating words, I have no fear.

I live to hear his unique music fall upon my EARS,

For people to believe he's dead brings to my eye a tear!

Immortality

Truly, he's one of the greatest men to ever LIVE,

To his cause, my life I've chosen to give.

For only those that are conscious, can really UNDERSTAND,

For Bob Marley was a godsend to humanity and music and truly didn't need a band!

Dedicated to: Bob Marley

15

Reproach

For in unimaginable darkness lies his SOUL,

To follow the rapper is his main goal.

Of himself, he has no CONTROL,

On him, evil threatens to take a toll!

Their potential for worthy greatness, Hip-Hop SMOTHERS,

Having little or no self-knowledge, how can this group care about another?

Insensitive, are they to the mourning of the youth's MOTHERS,

Revolutionized, must become the entertainer for Africa's redemption to be furthered.

No longer should the youth mimic the rapper, I dub as the evil OTHER!

Reproach

Without a paddle, the rapper would like to send me downstream,

As Malcolm uttered, we've experienced the American nightmare, not the DREAM.

Materialism is what these imbeciles hold dear,

And of the omnipotent, they seem to have no FEAR.

To Lucifer and not JAH, they incline their ears!

What profits a man if he gains the whole world, but doesn't find the creator HERE?

Reproach

The greatest destruction of the African youth,

Is none other than the rapper, if you want to know the TRUTH!

Some often wonder how this group came to dominate,

The enlightened one's have sat by idle and let this madness ESCALATE.

Now at an unbelievable momentum our children and communities the rapper devastates!

From this doom, only the ALMIGHTY and true knowledge can EMANCIPATE,

The conscious better declare war against the entertainer before it's too LATE!

Notes: I am condemning the negative and materialistic rap! Not the small portion of rap that is positive and educational!

16

Realism

Most are still begging and pleading for JUSTICE....

Truly, it'll never be granted freely, at all,

And when harm or death becomes imminent most blacks STALL.

But, the soul constantly yearns to be free, so take heed to freedom's call.

Perhaps true fairness, we can one day ACQUIRE,

But only if black people start to make demands and cease to desire!

Realism

What have we not PAID?

What more could possibly be the cost?

The most precious thing being life, in which numerous Africans have LOST!

Realism

Are you too cowardly to jeopardize your life for what is next?

Permit yourself to see beyond the MASSES,

And then you'll be able to see on the other side of that that passes.

Notes: that that passes is material and Flesh!

17

This is for my People

Everyone is your EQUAL,

In reality, you are the chosen people.

Many more will have to DIE,

And any other belief is a mere lie.

The mothers are destined to WEEP,

Without their boys and men, will they have to learn to sleep.

This is for my People

Much more affliction and bloodshed, will we have to ENDURE,

Do you still want to be a part of the struggle, are you sure?

But, in the end, we will REJOICE,

To fight or die a slave, we have a choice.

Again, I could've sworn I just heard GOD and my ancestors VOICE!

This is for my People

We have to rid injustice of his place,

As Marcus Garvey often uttered, Up you mighty RACE!

To our past, did they wreak disaster,

But, of our future we have an opportunity to be MASTER.

Now, I petition JAH and my ancestors to direct,

Anything other than a new world, I will REJECT!

18

No longer am I a Slave

Back his name is what I gave,

The true way does knowledge PAVE.

For reading and praying, we were once beaten or sent to the grave.

But, to do this today, my people are FREE,

Unfortunately, of it they act terrified and flee!

From the grave our ancestors do SEE,

That wise and appreciative of their sacrifices we don't choose to be.

No longer am I a Slave

But, for my brothers and sisters I GRIEVE,

Behind their African culture and true identities they leave.

Content and bamboozled by what the white man told them to BELIEVE!

Will they ever awaken from their deep slumber?

If so, it'll be one small NUMBER!

At times, my blood does run cold,

Seeing that out to ignorance, they have SOLD.

Alone in the physical, I stand bold,

Knowing that in the spiritual, they encompass me, they that are of OLD!

Get into the Flow

On your face, disappointment you SHOW,
And about your life, more you would like to know,
However, you have not gotten into life's FLOW!
> Refuse to expect,
Capture the moment right now and the future NEGLECT,
Directing life and not believing in prospects!

Get into the Flow

Time is whom I take by the hand,
And life I try not to always COMMAND,
Instead, I befriend her and try to understand.

Get into the Flow

One may feel the wind, but can't determine which way it GOES,
An adventure it is meant to be though,
Life is quite empty when lived out of the FLOW.

20

One should take more seriously a Name

And for yourself you are to blame,

You must realize that things don't always remain the SAME.

Now is the time to take back your right,

Names used to have meaning and hidden power they did IGNITE,

Find yours and you'll come out of the darkness and into the light.

One should take more seriously a Name

To the Motherland, do I make my CALL,

The majority is void of their true culture, how can they stand tall?

Give the European back his name, for this is a start and not a FALL,

Let them know that you are serious about your heritage, once and for all!

To yourself, you, I must EXPOSE,

A name doesn't matter is the thought of those,

The one's in which the ancestors aren't CLOSE.

Their true selves they will never behold,

I recollect a proverb saying that a good name is more precious than GOLD.

Surly we must begin to honor and refrain from disgracing those of old!

Now proceed to discover your NAME,

Refuse to be the highest order of shame!

Wake up Everybody

Benighted as usual, happens to be the MULTITUDE,

A resolution to face the truth they won't conclude.

And as they continue to SLEEP,

The price that they'll pay when finally awakened will be even more steep.

And the youth are prone to go ASTRAY,

It's ironic to see one that will pray!

Wake up Everybody

Morals is something, very few KEEP,

No longer does it really affect one to behold another that weeps.

War is what man desires to WAGE,

For this is prophecy and we're living in the worst age.

Will the masses forever SNOOZE?

History reveals that the masses don't always remain fools,

But, with haste knowledge and righteousness must be what they CHOOSE.

22

Mental Slave

We are only free to ENTERTAIN,

In worldly affairs, they don't want us to use our brains.

And you brother, unconsciously utter this is SANE,

Because death is usually the gain.

As a freedman or woman, go to the GRAVE!

Remember how the freedom fighters behaved,

We had to fight for all we have, nothing was GAVE!

And everyone has a part in the road to pave,

But, one won't achieve it, by remaining a mental SLAVE

They can only kill the body, not the spirit, so be brave!

Mental Slave

Deep involvement in worldly affairs, they dare YOU,

To build our own nation, I really care too,

Mental slave, break the shackles and help me turn our grey skies BLUE!

And please break in pieces the chains without delay,

And capture freedom this very DAY!

Or in a grave without dignity, will you probably lay,

And don't you dare just PRAY!

Take action and help me GOD, is what you must say!

What is Due?

For it is really up to YOU,

Having only one life and not two,

You can really make your own dreams come TRUE!

Action always brought an effect, is the conclusion I drew,

Delighting in watching the bird as he FLEW,

Knowing that one that seeks always grew.

And his opportunities he never BLEW,

For himself he always set out to do.

What is Due?

Just go forth and be BRAVE,

And like a man behave.

Not a very desire, should be SAVED,

Go out and get what you want, because nothing will be gave!

Into your life, allow him to SHINE,

Believing that there isn't anything that can't be mine.

Behind, one must leave all doubt,

Whatever I believe is due you must SHOUT,

Knowing that faith and action is what it's all about!

24

Me, no one will MISTREAT,

Surly if one tries, he will suffer DEFEAT!

For you just can't always be kind,

Some will then take you to be BLIND,

Do good in spite of, must sometimes be left behind!

In some instances, the line one have to DRAW,

To be a fool should be against the law.

In my very self, a fool is what I once SAW,

But, when seen by yourself this is a fatal flaw!

Laughing at you, there will be MANY,

But, trials in the end, bring about plenty!

25

Arise

What about the racist COPS?

Having turned in the sheets for the uniforms, it must stop!

For a change, I do PLEAD,

There is nothing more that America needs.

Many will have to die and BLEED,

Because talk has never helped us to proceed.

To these revelations, please take HEED,

Of JAH, no longer must we be looked upon as the cursed seed!

Arise

We must construct our own NATION,

Denouncing the hypocrisy of the proclamation of emancipation!

A new people is what we have to BREED,

To render one's life to this struggle is the most worthy deed.

It's just no way that they could ever be our ALLY,

The truth about their past and present misdeeds they still deny.

Only a revolution will reconcile our differences, is my REPLY,

And as a free man, do I aim to die!

26

I am not Free

But, neither will I always remain in captivity!
I would rather die than let them control me,
Determined to fight like a man and not FLEE,
And in Mother Africa's bosom is where her children must be!
Only a dunce would deny this REALITY,
Into Africa's past, do I clearly see,
Blacks sprang from the most royal family TREE!

I am not Free

My people do they continue to enslave,
Perhaps we as a whole will only be free when we go to the GRAVE.
Most usually sit by idle and watch one or a few fight brave!
      And this is to no AVAIL,
These revolutionaries often die and their messages fail,
It takes the masses for a people to PREVAIL.
And from Africa, we was made to sit sail,
But, we must repatriate, because our mother WAILS!
Christ was a dread from Africa and in his hands they put nails!

27

We got it all Wrong

Everyone knows that death is a MUST,

Try not to mourn, if in JAH you trust,

For our bodies are nothing but DUST!

Solomon said, when one expires rejoice,

For to paradise you go, if you made the right CHOICE.

Only the body is silenced, the soul will perpetually have a voice!

Therefore, treat people the way, in which you wish to be TREATED,

And by guilt, when they cease to breathe, you won't be defeated,

By the soul of the deceased, you may even someday be GREETED!

We got it all Wrong

28

Reason

After I utter this, will I be accused of TREASON?
Fear nothing, my soul whispers during this season,
Our plight to them seems to be quite PLEASING.
Stand, I urge and take your right,
Liberty and respect usually takes a bloody FIGHT!
This is treason, they'll declare and die, I just might,
For saying that the American dream for Africans have been a FRIGHT.
And now, the hymn of martyrdom, I may soon have to recite!

Reason

What happened to the forty acres and the mule....

The biggest fabrication ever TOLD,
Granting others reparations, but not the African, how bold!
We suffered and died more than any group, but on that chapter the book they
FOLD.
That is why the revolution, her I will embrace tenderly and not just hold,
Into mental slavery countless are still being SOLD,
Loosen your shackles and heap on the dictator a heavy load!

Reason

Most don't even have a clue of their PLACE,

The veracity concerning Mother Africa they have no trace.

No wonder the cruel one can wreak shame on their FACE,

On reason, is how I plead my case!

29

Unappreciated

Of people, you don't find many that are so FOND,

As to give up their lives in hope that in a revolutionary way the people might respond.

In the event of this, among the people, they hope to bring a closer BOND!

Usually in death, the race tries to appreciate,

Why is it that they wait so LATE?

The significance of this phenomenon they opt to negate,

So much more, they could reap if they learn to APPRECIATE.

Unappreciated

To really know the value of these messiahs is grand,

If most would only take the time to try to UNDERSTAND,

Opening their hearts instead of their hands.

My prayer is that more will soon COMPREHEND,

Because this nature of mortal, everyday Allah don't send,

Come and behold reality and cease to PRETEND!

Facade

The smile I wear isn't GENUINE,

My moderation, do the injustices undermine.

What a brilliant plan did Willie Lynch PERPETRATE,

Brother it's him not me that you should hate.

Everywhere I look among us there is STRIFE,

My people would rather kill me than take the oppressors life!

Sometimes the folly causes me to laugh like a CLOWN,

Laughter temporarily relieves, so in sorrow I don't drown!

But, a short while after, I find myself with a FROWN.

Facade

Don't believe everything that is shown,

My life I'm determined to dictate on my OWN.

All throughout the earth has the pale face flown,

Only to return to the earth where a revolution is certain to be FULL- BLOWN!

Epilogue

My hope is that I was able to attract a great audience.

I am grateful for the seen and unseen influences. For this work was not orchestrated to gain currency. Instead, it was composed for my love of poetry and people but primary for my FATHER'S will. It will have served it's purpose if only one read or hear the words contained in this work that called for hard and constant labor, and act in a manner that is gratifying to the MASTER who resides in the celestial. One must realize the potency of words. For the dictionary should become one of your best and cherished companions.

Mainly self-taught I am. I have received acknowledgements from several high profile individuals. Not that this makes me an authority, but I believe I have a lot to share that could help the world. For I would still be someone with or without the recognition from them. Nevertheless, the acknowledgements do serve to encourage, confirm, and enforce what I have been feeling inside for quite sometime.

There are more occurrences and experiences I didn't disclose and they continue to multiply! Everyday of my new life has become an adventure! However, all praise is to JAH! I could do nothing without him and I am nothing without him. I have obtained all this favor by his grace and my effort. I perform these works for his GLORY! I pray and hope that all enjoyed and learnt something from my STORY!

For this is merely the beginning of
the dawn of greater works to come!